Let Us Go On to Maturity

LET US GO ON
TO MATURITY

by
JOHN E. HUNTER

ZONDERVAN PUBLISHING HOUSE
A DIVISION OF THE ZONDERVAN CORPORATION
GRAND RAPIDS, MICHIGAN

"Therefore leaving the principles of the doctrine of Christ, *let us go on to maturity.*"
(Hebrews 6:1)

CONTENTS

CHAPTER 1

THE RISEN CHRIST

THE WEEK I ARRIVED in America during the summer of 1966 I received an urgent phone call from a Christian leader in a nearby town. He said there was a state college in their area and just two weeks before, one of the professors had spoken at a luncheon meeting for all interested students. He had taken as his theme "God is Dead." He had brought all manner of forceful philosophy to prove his point. The following week the college newspaper had given his message a big write-up on the front page. The entire experience had caused much unpleasantness in the surrounding community. This college had begun upon a Christian foundation and this attack on the faith from one of the faculty seemed too much for the townspeople to take. There was also a small, struggling Christian group among the students and this open attack had proved demoralizing to their witness.

So it was that the Christian leader asked me if I could go to the college one lunch hour that week and speak in answer to such an open attack. I was both free and willing to stand alongside those who were fighting this battle on their own campus. We arrived to find a large gathering of students plus some townspeople. The professor himself was also in the audience.

I began by saying that, although I had been invited to speak as a result of the "God is Dead" lecture, I had no intention of arguing the case or even discussing the

11

idea. I was not interested in considering a God who was dead—I had come to speak about a Christ who was alive, One who said, "I am he that liveth, and was dead; and, behold, I am alive for evermore" (Revelation 1:18).

We then considered logically and factually the tremendous truth of the resurrection of Christ. I read for them I Corinthians 15:1-11 and showed them the detailed list of witnesses who had seen the risen Christ. We saw how, in verse 6, it is recorded that, at that time, there were about five hundred people who had seen the Lord—all at the same time. It would have been possible, when the letter was written, to have checked with witness after witness regarding the personal appearance and behavior of the risen Lord—the entire incident was a historical fact.

In the early part of this present century a group of lawyers and legal men in London, England, met together to discuss the evidence for the actual resurrection of the Lord Jesus. They wished to see if there was sufficient evidence which would be acceptable in an English court of law. When all their deliberations were ended they came up with this considered opinion, that there was sufficient evidence to make the resurrection of Christ one of the best accepted facts of ancient history.

We followed with a discussion of the fact that the resurrection of Christ was not just an isolated incident with nothing else to support it. I showed them a small book called *Countdown* by G. B. Hardy, published by the Moody Press.* (I hoped that many might purchase a copy for themselves.) Mr. Hardy is really communicating with the college age when he writes in such a pointed, acceptable manner. On page 25, speaking of a definition of religion, he writes: "There are but two essential requirements:

* Used by permission of Moody Press, Moody Bible Institute, Chicago.

1. Has any one cheated death and proved it?
2. Is it available to me?

Here is the complete record:

    Confucius' tomb—occupied
    Buddha's tomb—occupied
    Mohammed's tomb—occupied
    Jesus' tomb—EMPTY

Argue as you will . . . THERE IS NO POINT IN FOL-LOWING A LOSER." Mr. Hardy then goes on to present a wonderful fact which has thrilled the hearts of true Christians through the ages. In the Old Testament there are approximately three hundred passages where we can read incidents and details pertaining to the Christ, the Messiah who was to come. This is historical fore-knowledge, where God has guided the writers to record the names of places and actions and incidents hundreds of years before they ever happened. This is not a matter of philosophy or clever human speculation or supposition, but a plain statement of fact, clear and logical and capable of no human explanation. All three hundred items of prophecy, or historical foreknowledge came true in the life of the Lord Jesus Christ.

Some critics, in their attempts to find an explanation, suggest that the Lord Jesus deliberately arranged to fulfill these incidents. In suggesting this they most sure-ly prove the deity of Christ, because no one but God could have fulfilled such "arrangements."

Consider the following items of historical foreknowl-edge with the Old Testament references and the New Testament fulfillment:

Born of a virgin—Isaiah 7:14; Matthew 1:22, 23
In the family of David—Isaiah 11:1; Luke 1:32
Born at Bethlehem—Micah 5:2; Matthew 2:4-6
The massacre of the children—Jeremiah 31:15; Mat-thew 2:16-18
Carried to Egypt and the return—Hosea 11:1; Mat-thew 2:15

13

Anointed of the Spirit—Isaiah 61:1, 2; Luke 4:17-21

Entry into Jerusalem on an ass—Zechariah 9:9; Matthew 21:4, 5

Betrayed by His intimate friend—Psalm 41:9; John 13:18

Forsaken by His disciples—Zechariah 13:6; Matthew 26:31

Sold for thirty pieces of silver— Zechariah 11:12, 13; and the story of the Potters' field—Matthew 26: 15; 27:3-10

The spitting and the buffeting—Isaiah 50:6, Matthew 27:30

The gall and the vinegar—Psalm 69:21; Matthew 27:34, 48

Not one bone broken—Exodus 12:46; John 19:33, 36

His feet and hands pierced—Psalm 22:16; John 20:25

His garments divided by lot—Psalm 22:18; John 19:23, 24

Malefactors and rich men—Isaiah 53:9; Matthew 27: 38, 57-60

Consider for a moment, as an example, the prophecy in Zechariah 11:12, 13—"They weighed for my price thirty pieces of silver . . . And I took the thirty pieces of silver, and cast them to the potter in the house of the LORD." The first half we can see fulfilled in Matthew 26:15—"What will ye give me, and I will deliver him unto you? And they covenanted with him for thirty pieces of silver." But whoever could conceive of a situation where a man would take thirty pieces of silver and throw them to the floor in the house of the Lord! Imagine throwing a handful of silver along the floor of the temple! Yet Matthew 27:5 says—"and he cast down the pieces of silver in the temple," an amazing, literal fulfillment of what was foretold hundreds of years before.

14

The most remarkable fulfillment of prophecy was the literal resurrection of Christ from the dead. Each of the three hundred foretellings in the Old Testament became facts in the New Testament. Professor W. Stoner, M.S., with the endorsement of the American Scientific Affiliation, has estimated that for the Lord Jesus to have fulfilled these prophecies purely by chance could be expressed mathematically as one chance in 10^{181} or 10 with a hundred and eighty more zeros added on. What a number—what a chance—what a Saviour!

The resurrection of the Lord Jesus is not only an accepted historical fact, but a fact proved so by the culminating fulfillment of the historical foreknowledge of God.

When that luncheon meeting had ended many of the students were impressed by the logic of the Word of God compared to the "inspired" philosophy of a defeated generation. The local radio station had taped the entire message and this was played back several times that week over the air.

But, may I ask, What does the resurrection of Christ mean to you? What impact does it have on your daily life? Is it just a historical event, an item of your faith— or is it such that your entire life begins anew with this glorious fact? What part does the risen Christ play in your daily confrontation with the mounting pressures experienced on every hand? The tragedy today is that many Christians live as if the Lord never rose from the dead. They know their sins are forgiven, that they are going to heaven when they die because He died on the cross, but, in the meantime, they face the hopeless struggle of trying to cope with events and circumstances that reduce them to hopeless failures. The resurrection of Christ is an item present in their belief but absent in their behavior.

The wonderful fact we can go on to share in this chapter is that the resurrection achieved two dramatic ends. First, the resurrection of Christ *fulfilled all the prophecies of God*. Second, the resurrection of Christ *released all the promises of God*. This risen Lord is the One who makes possible our utter and complete enjoyment of the glorious promises of God hidden away in the Word of God. It is the enjoyment of these promises that makes possible a life where sin is restrained, temptation is resisted, fear is neutralized, and anxiety and depression lose their power.

Take, as an example, the precious words of God in Isaiah 26:3, "Thou wilt keep him in perfect peace, whose mind is stayed on thee: because he trusteth in thee." Put these words alongside verses 12 and 13 of the same chapter and see the greatest missing experience in the world today—a sense of deep, abiding, inward, personal peace. The generation in which we live is lashing itself into a crazy turmoil of passion, excitement, fear and hostility coupled with a senseless infatuation with pleasure and noiseful living.

Yet, there continues to be a deep, deep, longing for peace; for that inner peace that soothes away the hurt and brings a restful calm to the tired personality. The risen Christ has made all this possible in our experience. He is utterly relevant to the crying needs of young and old. He has released all God's promises. This peace can be ours when His presence is real in our hearts and lives.

There are two glorious promises in Isaiah 42:1-3 that could bring wondrous blessing today to any person hungry enough to receive all that God gives—in Christ, the risen Christ. See how it begins—"Behold my servant, whom I uphold; mine elect, in whom my soul delighteth; I have put my spirit upon him: he shall bring forth judgment to the Gentiles." This last phrase is better translated—"he shall reveal truth to the nations"— something the Lord Jesus can do for us. In verse 3 we find a twofold promise that can be experienced through the risen Lord. The first phrase reads—"A bruised reed shall he not break." This is a lovely word picture of the relationship of the Lord Jesus to a poor, helpless, lost sinner.

I lived for fifteen years in a farming community in the midst of rich fertile fields. I came to realize that the presence of reeds in a field was a sign of damp, acid soil. Such an area of ground would be useless for raising crops. It was wasteland until time and money had been spent dealing with the soil condition. Therefore, a reed is really a useless plant and it grows in a waste place. Now put this information into verse 3 and you find that "a bruised reed" is a useless plant, in a waste place, in a damaged condition. What a vivid description this is of many lives today—useless—in a wasted area—bruised and damaged by sin and circumstance.

Now notice what is the reaction of the risen Lord to such a case of abject want—"A bruised reed shall he not break." The world will ignore or reject or destroy such a pathetic failure, but not so the risen Christ. He can make the waste place to blossom like the rose. He can bring forgiveness of sin, cleansing from guilt, and through His own indwelling Spirit, the peace of God that irons out all the wrinkles of a creased and crushed personality. This is how the risen Lord makes true the promise of God for the needy sinner who is "without Christ . . . having no hope . . . without God in the world" (Ephesians 2:12).

The first promise in verse 3 was for a poor tired sinner. The second promise is for a poor tired saint— "the smoking flax shall he not quench." This is another word picture that takes for its example the simple oil lamp used in the Middle East, even to this day. The container is a small boat-shaped vessel made of clay or metal. The front of the lamp is pinched together leaving a small hole into which a piece of twisted flax is inserted. This then acts as the wick. The lamp is filled with oil, into which the twisted flax reaches. The oil is then

17

drawn up the flax so that the wick becomes saturated with the oil. When a flame is applied to the protruding section of the flax it ignites and continues to burn with a soft warm glow. This is the simple principle under which the eastern lamp operates. It is easy to see that the lamp can function only as long as there is oil either in the vessel or saturating the flax. It is necessary to make sure that such oil is always present.

However, the time could arise when the oil had not been replenished. If this should happen the vessel would go dry and the flax would go dry as the saturating oil was gradually consumed. There would thus be a flame, but no oil to burn. What would happen next is the word picture in this verse—there would be a "smoking flax." The oil would burn with a warm soft light, but the flax would burn with an acrid smoke. The lamp, instead of giving comfort and illumination, would simply give off a smoke screen offensive to the nose, hurtful to the eyes and useless in its performance.

The immediate reaction would be to quench the flax, to stop it from causing discomfort to those around. But—"a smoking flax shall he not quench." The risen Christ is God's answer not only for the tired sinner, but also for the tired saint. There are many sincere and earnest Christians who today are struggling hard to live for Jesus. They want to be a true answer to the word of Christ—"Ye are the light of the world" (Matthew 5:14). There they are, each one a twist of flax, each one in his own appointed place, but each one trying to burn for Jesus. How simple is the lesson of the lamp— it isn't the flax that burns but the oil!

The flax can only smoke, giving off a witness of its own ability to cause discomfort and distress. All that is needed is "Give me oil in my lamp, keep me burning." Oil throughout the Bible is a type and picture of the Holy Spirit, thus the illustration of the lamp completely demonstrates the basic truth in living the Christian

18

life—my Christian life is not what I can do for Jesus but what He can do through me.

All I can do as a sincere, hard-working twist of flax is to smoke, whereby I consume my own potentiality and throw no light on the surrounding darkness—I simply add to and become part of that darkness! But when I realize that "the smoking flax shall he not quench," the entire situation can change immediately. Other people may wish to quench me. Quite rightly so, for I would be a constant offense and embarrassment, but not so the risen Lord.

As I recognize the truth of His Holy Spirit indwelling me and learn once again that He is the light of the world, then, as I allow the risen Lord to fill me and possess me and control me, the capacity to shine is fully restored. It would be good to realize that a smoking flax would need to be trimmed before it could give a clear light once more. Trimming is simply the removal of a burned-out self so that the oil can flow freely through the twist of flax. Incidentally, an oil lamp, when it is functioning perfectly, still needs to be trimmed at regular intervals so that no burned-out self will interfere with the work of the oil.

As we move on now into this book we will be thinking constantly of these wonderful truths—that the risen Christ is God's answer to all our needs—that He not only fulfilled the prophecies of God but He also made real all the glorious promises of God—that the quality of our Christian life is our response to these facts.

A PRAYER FOR MEDITATION

Thank You, Heavenly Father, for such a wonderful salvation.

Thank You that the Lord Jesus in all His risen power is the answer to all my need.

Thank You for His precious blood shed for me on

Calvary's cross, so that my sins might be completely dealt with.

As I have appropriated His death FOR *me, so may I appropriate His risen life in me.*

May the desert blossom as a rose and may the light shine clear and true as I yield my heart and life to be filled, possessed and controlled by His Holy Spirit. In Jesus' name. Amen.

CHAPTER 2

THE PROBLEM OF CHRISTIAN MATURITY

As WE READ AND STUDY the books in the Bible we can
often assume that these are books of a bygone age
written to people long since dead and buried. But, if we
turn to I Corinthians 1:2, we find that not only is this
letter addressed to people who lived in Corinth hundreds of years ago, it is also for "all that in every place
call upon the name of Jesus Christ our Lord, both
theirs and ours." We thus find ourselves intimately involved in this powerful letter. What it had to say to the
Corinthians, it says to us today—in comfort, challenge
and rebuke.

A closer examination of verse 2 gives us a threefold
picture of these Corinthians of long ago. They were . . .
*the church of God . . . sanctified in Christ Jesus . . .
called saints.* This is indeed a wonderful appellation
and brings to our imagination a group of people who
were holy, dedicated, living strong, triumphant Christian lives. Our first reaction is to hesitate before moving
any closer. These are special people, super-saints, and
we are not worthy to associate with them, even though
the same verse unites us in "Jesus Christ our Lord,
both theirs and ours."

However, it is good to realize that this threefold
designation is what they were in the presence of God.
Positionally, this was their standing, and it was all
through the infinite grace of God. They were the
Church, the called-out ones. They were sanctified in

Christ Jesus, but this was not anything they had achieved, this was the work of the Holy Spirit. They were also saints. This is no reference to holy statues or stained glass windows; to somber individuals with halos around their heads. The teaching is that they had been made holy in the sight of God.

In like manner we, too, are the Church of God; we, too, have been sanctified in Christ Jesus and, by the boundless mercy of God we are saints—not because of the quality of the lives we live, but because of the quality of the death that Jesus died.

This then was their standing in the sight of God, but what was their standing in the sight of the people among whom they lived and worked and moved? If we turn to I Corinthians 3:1-3 we find quite a different picture. Verse 1 says: "And I, brethren, could not speak unto you as unto spiritual, but as unto carnal, even as unto babes in Christ." They were still ... sanctified in Christ Jesus ... called saints, in the sight of God, but what a different situation this chapter reveals. Paul could address them as brethren, but they were not spiritual. They were carnal, which means they were living the old life where self was in complete control.

Verse 3 describes how this carnal life was showing itself, "there is among you envying, and strife, and divisions." Their beliefs were one thing, but their behavior was quite something else. Notice the progression from envying, which is thoughts in operation, to strife, which is words in operation, to end up in divisions, which are deeds in operation. The entire development of thought, word and deed is here revealed in these Corinthian Christians.

Verse 1 designates them as *babes in Christ*. From this we gather that they had been born again. They had life with all the potential of glorious future development for Christ. They possessed the capacity to be all that God wanted them to be—but they were still babes in Christ. They had been saved by the blood of Christ through the infinite grace of God—but then they had stopped in their Christian experience.

They were "saved and stuck." Possessing everything from God, they had achieved nothing for God. They were living the same kind of miserable defeated lives that they had lived before they ever came to Christ— even though they were ... *the church of God ... sanctified in Christ Jesus ... called saints.* Now, see the point of this letter which is addressed not only to them, but also to us! We need to search our hearts and see if we have this ungodly progression of envy, strife and division operating through thought, word and deed. Have we been born again only to remain as babes in Christ?

Babies are sweet and precious when God sends them into our families. How helpless they are! They are dependent upon us for every item of daily living, every moment of every day. But this we gladly undertake because we know that, in God's good time, the helpless babe will not only cry, but creep and crawl and then go on into those fascinating ages of three, four and five. Then on into youth and older years when all the baby helplessness is past and gone. This is our hope, and when it is fulfilled we praise God for His great goodness.

But sometimes, just sometimes, the baby does not go on to develop as the rest do. Some unseen, unknown mental limitation causes development to slow down or even to stop. What a heartache this can be to the parents who find that their baby is always going to be a baby—whatever age or size may develop. What was precious now becomes a problem, and, although God by His great mercy can provide strength sufficient for the task, there is a sense of pathetic loneliness and a lack of fulfillment. When babies stay babies someone has to undertake in new and heartsearching ways.

This, in a measure, was the problem in Corinth. The Corinthian Christians had been born again, they had

23

received life through Christ Jesus, but something had entered to arrest the development of these young Christians. This was a resurgence of the old way of life, the carnal nature was demonstrating itself in their envy and strife and division.

I Corinthians 5:1, 2 reveals another area where their complete failure was shown. "It is reported commonly that there is fornication [sexual looseness] among you." Notice the word *commonly*. This was an open sin for all the world to gaze at, but no one in the church had been moved to judge it and put a stop to the moral cancer in their midst. The pagans had been shocked by such sexual depravity, but not the church. These people were still *the church of God . . . sanctified in Christ Jesus . . . called saints*, but what a mockery they were making of their faith.

It hardly seems possible that people can be Christians and still be engaged in any form of sexual looseness—until we look around us today and see how low the moral standards are falling not only in the world but in the Church itself. This is not only so among those of high school or college age, but also among older Christians. Areas of sexual looseness are reported and find their way to the newspaper, unless influence is brought to bear to keep such a "scandal" out of the court of the social conscience.

Why is this so? Why do people today become involved in such wretched and miserable practices? One of the answers is that they have never grown up in the faith. They have been content to be saved and to know they are going to heaven when they die. They miss the glorious experience of going on with Christ. They somehow assume that God's salvation consists only of having forgiveness of sins and an assurance of heaven.

This is sad because no one benefits by their ignorance—except the devil. They themselves are irresponsible, unsatisfied and so useless in the faith. They, being babes in Christ, make so much work for other people.

Not only can they not assume places of leadership and responsibility, but they display all the emotional instability of a babe and need special care and additional patience as they limp through life—a constant casualty on the hands of pastor and people.

Chapter 6 has one more thing to say about these people who were "saved and stuck." A further example of their carnal ways and of their baby-like behavior is seen in verses 1-8. Here Paul is reproving them for failing to settle their quarrels in the sight of God. In verse 5 he says, "I speak to your shame"; in verse 7, "Now therefore there is utterly a fault among you, because ye go to law one with another." These Christians had been taking cases into the pagan law courts which should have been settled in humility in the presence of God. They had been accusing one another, defaming and dragging one another before the spotlight of pagan power—just to prove a point or to get even.

These three chapters make sad reading as we measure up the emptiness and the fruitless lives in the Corinthian church of those days—and all because they were babes in Christ. They had enough faith to come to the cross and trust Christ for salvation, but not enough to realize that, "he which hath begun a good work in you will finish it" (Philippians 1:6).

Let us remember that this letter is also written to us today. God began the good work in our lives. Is it continuing? If so, who is in charge of "Operation Completion"? There is one thing we can say regarding the background of the Corinthian Christians—they lived in one of the most wicked cities that ever existed. Corinth was one of the sin centers of the ancient world. On every hand they would see sin and sex and violence.

The Corinthians had also been raised in the darkness of this paganism. This was to them the only life they had ever known. But what was true for them is also true of many young Christians today, who, having been raised in a culture based on sin, sex and violence, have now to live a Christian life against such a background of pressure on every hand. The challenge in this letter is—Am I still a babe in Christ? Do I need to grow up in my faith?

There is a world of contrast between the epistles to the Corinthians and the epistle to the Hebrews. As we have seen, the Corinthians had a pagan background, steeped in all the vice and impurity of that wicked city. The letter to the Hebrews was written to people of another "world," another culture, whose moral fiber was based on the majestic glory of the Law and whose one aim was to keep themselves unspotted from Gentile contamination. Jehovah was their God and they were His people, and the rest of the world was a thing apart.

We saw that the Corinthians were addressed as, *"sanctified in Christ Jesus . . . called saints."* If we turn to Hebrews 3:1 we see how the writer there greets them as, *"holy brethren, partakers of the heavenly calling."* Notice again the dignity of these words. They were holy brethren—consecrated and set apart for God. They were partakers of the heavenly calling—they had a share in all the glorious promises and wondrous potential of the outreaching plan of God.

Here were a people truly prepared by race and relationship to God, to go out and do exploits for God. But when we turn to Hebrews 5:10 - 6:3 we find an unusual comment on their reaction to this glorious relationship. In verse 10 the writer was beginning a Bible study on the Lord Jesus as, "an high priest after the order of Melchisedec." He interrupts this study to say, in verse 11, "Of whom we have many things to say, and hard to be uttered, seeing ye are dull of hearing!" What an abrupt statement—*ye are dull of hearing!* Who were dull of hearing? *The holy brethren, partakers of the heavenly calling.*

He goes on in verse 12, "For when for the time ye ought to be teachers, ye have need that one teach you

26

again." Not only were they dull of hearing, they were dull of doing, dull of teaching, dull of witnessing, dull of serving and being out on the job for the Lord. Verse 12 continues this penetrating analysis by asserting that they had become so needy and helpless in their lives, they needed milk and only milk. Strong meat, the implications and teaching of the fuller Word of God, was too much for them. Verse 13 says that because they were at the milk stage they were mere babes in Christ. The *Amplified Bible* gives, "For every one who continues to feed on milk is obviously inexperienced *and* unskilled in the doctrine of righteousness, [that is, of conformity to the divine will in purpose, thought and action,] for he is a mere infant—not able to talk yet!"

The Holy Spirit uses stronger words still in verse 14, indicating that they were not full-grown, because those who were really adult in their faith were those, "who by reason of use have their senses exercised to discern both good and evil." This is certainly a penetrating analysis by God's Holy Spirit into a people who were *holy brethren, partakers of the heavenly calling.*

See how it begins with their dullness of hearing. They had not allowed the Word of God to enter their personal lives. It was so satisfying, outwardly, to be known as holy brethren and to take pride in their heavenly calling—but it led nowhere.

Their behavior reflected their lack of involvement with God's Word. There was no dynamic for service and no discernment between good and evil. Once again, as with the Corinthians, the same charge is leveled at them—they were babes in Christ. They had been born again, they had Life, but they, too, were "saved and stuck."

Notice the comparison with the Corinthians. The ex-pagan believers were babes because of the things they *did*—the envy, strife and divisions—the sexual immorality—the vindictiveness in the law courts. These Hebrew Christians were babes because of the things

27

they did *not* do. This is indicated especially in 6:1—"Therefore leaving the principles [the A.B.C.'s] of the doctrine of Christ, let us go on unto perfection."

The one cure for their problem is here stated so clearly—*let us go on unto perfection.* It is good at this point to make sure that we fully understand the meaning of the word *perfection.* This is no idealistic dream impossible of attainment—the better translation of the word *perfection* is "maturity." *Let us go on to maturity.*

What these Hebrew Christians needed more than all else was to grow up, to allow the Word of God to challenge them, teach them, possess them until they were mature. We thus see that although the Corinthian Christians and Hebrew Christians were different in many ways—the same spiritual complaint was made about them—they were babes in Christ.

This period of prolonged babyhood had been the result of different backgrounds, situations and circumstances—but one remedy was prescribed for both, they needed to go on to maturity. Living in a world full of opposition and persecution they needed muscles on their faith and strength to stand and withstand the pressures of a pagan world.

Having challenged them severely in Hebrews 5, the writer goes on in 6:9-12 to comfort them. He says, "But, beloved, we are persuaded better things of you, and things that accompany salvation, though we thus speak." Notice that intriguing phrase—*things that accompany salvation.*

My salvation is not only an end in itself, there are also many wonderful things that should accompany my salvation. These had been absent so far in the experience of these Hebrew Christians. Verses 11 and 12 present a precious admonition from the Lord, "and we desire that every one of you do shew the same diligence to the full assurance of hope unto the end: That ye be not slothful, but followers of them who through faith and patience inherit the promises."

There had been laziness in their lives, dullness and a lack of fruitfulness for God, but now things were going to change. They were going on to maturity. There would be many exciting things accompanying their salvation. Best of all they were going on through faith and patience to inherit the promises of God, here and now, in their daily experience.

This thought links us with the first chapter of our book—the risen Christ not only fulfilled all the prophecies of God, He released and made possible all the promises of God. So the promises they were going to inherit would all find their fulfillment in an increasing knowledge and a deeper relationship with the risen Lord Jesus.

Such was the Word of God for the Hebrews as well as for the Corinthians. And, of course, the whole point of this challenge is that it comes to us with the same authority as it came to them. So many Christians today are "saved and stuck." They have been born again, their sins are forgiven, they are on their way to heaven —but they are still babes in Christ, they have never grown in the faith.

They may be babes because of the things they do— as in Corinth. They may be babes because of what they do not do—as with the Hebrews. Whatever the cause, the result is the same—an experience of prolonged babyhood with all its attendant limitations, frustrations and utter uselessness in the things of God.

If only Christian men and women would go on to maturity, and experience power in their daily lives and a robust quality of vigorous endurance, what a change would come over our churches. The pagan world around us would be challenged by lives inexplicable, but so desirable in their capacity to handle sin and sorrow, temptation and turmoil.

The need is present in all our hearts and lives, and

the answer to that need is available to all who will go on to maturity. How wonderful it would be if, as we read this book, God should unlock to us the door that leads to Christian maturity.

A PRAYER FOR MEDITATION

Thank You, Heavenly Father, that there is an answer to fear and failure and frustration.

Thank You that I do not need to go on as a babe in Christ. How wonderful to realize that through Your Word I can grow and find a new quality of Christian maturity.

Create in me a new desire to go on into the truth of Your Word.

As I read this book may the Lord Jesus become increasingly real to me in thought and word and deed.

May I be ready to hear and quick to obey—for Jesus' sake. Amen.

CHAPTER 3

JOSHUA—GOD'S PLAN

WE SAW IN OUR first chapter that the resurrection of Christ achieved two dramatic ends. First, the resurrection of Christ fulfilled all the prophecies of God. Second, the resurrection of Christ released and made possible all the promises of God. This is seen especially in II Corinthians 1:20 where we read, "For all the promises of God in him are yea, and in him Amen, unto the glory of God." The *Amplified Bible* gives this, "For as many as are the promises of God, they all find their Yes (answer) in Him (Christ)."

Consider the lovely and simple meaning of this truth. Wherever we find a precious promise of God in the Bible, one that holds out blessing, encouragement and guidance, we can say to ourselves, "Is this true for me, really true today?" The answer comes back every time, "Yes, indeed it is true, for all God's promises find their Yes in Christ."

We sometimes sing a chorus, "Christ is the answer to my every need," and how blessedly true this is. But more than being the answer to my need, He is also the answer to God's eternal promises. When we realize that most of these promises are safely hidden in the Old Testament, this gives us a further incentive to look therein to discover the treasury of God.

Another reason for turning to the Old Testament is found in the passage, I Corinthians 10:1-12. Here we have it clearly stated that we are to look back to the events surrounding the story of the adventures of the children of Israel on their journey from Egypt to the Promised Land of Canaan.

Their reactions to the promises of God are to be, to us, a source of warning and clear instruction. Verse 6 says, "Now these things were our examples [our warnings and admonitions.]" Verse 11 says, "Now all these things happened unto them for ensamples: and they are written for our admonition." The word "ensamples" means—as types or figures—as examples and warnings to us. "For our admonition" means to fit us for right action by good instruction.

God gave the Israelites many promises. The land of Canaan was called the Promised Land. Their reaction to the promises of God was their very history. Everything depended upon whether they accepted or rejected the promises of God. In like manner my Christian life, the quality of life that I live, is dependent to a large extent upon my response to the promises of God.

God's Word has taught us that our Lord Jesus is God's eternal "Yes" to every promise, so that all we have to do is to turn the potential of promise into the power of experience. This we do every time we experience the sufficiency of Christ in any situation or need or crisis.

We can be helped along this line of thinking if we do exactly what I Corinthians 10:1-12 tells us. Let us turn back to the Book of Joshua and see this very subject being demonstrated in the life and experience of this one man.

Notice the title of this book, it is "The Book of Joshua"—the story of a man's life shown in his response to the promises of God. In like manner you are writing "The Book of You"—whatever your name may be. Your life story is being most surely recorded in the secretariat of heaven, and the daily report is not so much the problems and situations that arise, but the way you respond to such events.

The promises of God are the powerhouse of blessing, the eternal tools of God whereby victories are won and character is carved out of the bedrock of human experience. And remember, every promise is available, nothing is withheld, because the Lord Jesus Christ is God's "Yes" to every question arising from the promises of His Word.

In this day, with its great emphasis on young people, we are inclined to think that youth has almost a prerogative to the opportunities of service for God. "Too old at forty" is more than a catch phrase, and some Christians can be tempted to make increasing age an excuse for holding back in their involvement for God.

The Book of Joshua comes as an immediate challenge to such an idea. Joshua was a man who lived in Egypt in the days of bondage and who was old enough, when the Israelites came out, to be sent as a member of the search party to spy out the Promised Land. Then for forty years he lived in the wilderness before he became the hero of the Book of Joshua.

Joshua 24:29 tells us that he was a hundred and ten when he died, so we can see quite clearly that when his real life story began he was well over forty years old. Possibly he was between sixty and seventy.

Joshua 1 begins with quite an abrupt statement. The first words God said to Joshua were, "Moses my servant is dead." In a way, this would come as a blow. Deuteronomy 34:7 says, "and Moses was an hundred and twenty years old when he died: his eye was not dim, nor his natural force abated."

Moses had not been ill, he was not suffering in any way. Deuteronomy 34:1 records that Moses went up from the plains of Moab to the top of Pisgah and while he was there he died and the Lord buried him, "but no man knoweth of his sepulchre unto this day" (verse 6). Moses had made many ascents of mountains before to meet with God, and in God's time he had returned to his people. The children of Israel were used to this behavior, but this time he never came back.

They were waiting, but nothing happened. Then we read in Joshua 1, "Now after the death of Moses the servant of the LORD it came to pass that the LORD spake unto Joshua the son of Nun, Moses' minister, saying, Moses my servant is dead." He wasn't coming back any more, and this is where the Book of Joshua begins, with one man's reaction to responsibility.

This was going to mean a totally new life for Joshua. For the last forty years he had been Moses' minister—Moses' servant—taking orders and assisting his master in the colossal task of guiding this great crowd of wanderers. Moses was called the servant of God and Joshua was the servant of Moses. We can see from verses 6, 7 and 9 that the first reaction of Joshua was one of fear, and of utter inability to face up to, and cope with, such a situation.

Joshua had not made a decision for forty years; he had simply done as Moses commanded, and now he was being called upon to assume the leadership of several millions of people. No wonder his heart was filled with fear! It was not that he was a coward, far from it. His was the natural reaction to the office of leadership after so many years of quiet obedience.

He would also be apprehensive concerning the children of Israel. No one would know more than Joshua about the heartaches and sorrows of Moses. There must have been many occasions when Moses returned to his tent with a broken heart over the wretched treatment he had received from the people whom he was seeking to lead and serve. Deuteronomy 31:27 records some searching words spoken by Moses to this same people, "For I know thy rebellion, and thy stiff neck: behold, while I am yet alive with you this day, ye have been rebellious against the LORD; and how much more after my death?"

These words would rise again in the memory of

Joshua—*how much more after my death?* They would break Joshua's heart as they had broken the heart of Moses. The people would murmur and complain and be completely ungrateful for whatever was done for them. No wonder Joshua faced the news of Moses' death with fear, anxiety, and real trepidation.

Now notice that this is how the Book of Joshua begins—with a man caught up in circumstances that frighten him and baffle him. This may be how the "Book of You" is beginning. Perhaps you, too, are frightened, frustrated and baffled by what appears to lie before you. See then the great value of this book to your own heart, especially in the first nine verses.

God's reaction to Joshua's fear was to give him a threefold plan on which he would step out to experience victory and blessing. God gave Joshua—A Promise—A Program—A Power—and his response to this threefold gift is the story of the Book of Joshua.

In like manner, as we realize that every promise of God finds its answer in Christ, we too can write the book of our own life against the same threefold plans of God. As we see our experience and enjoyment of Christ as God's "Promise" and "Program" and "Power" for us, then the way to a new life swings open for each one of us.

The "Promise" God gave to Joshua was a wonderful twofold promise seen in 1:3 and 5. In verse 3 we read, "Every place that the sole of your foot shall tread upon, that have I given unto you as I said unto Moses." Notice, first, the two tenses in the verse, *your foot shall tread upon.* This is a reference to every future experience. Then comes, *that have I given unto you.* This is a guarantee of past assurance—I have already given it to you.

In other words, God was giving Joshua a promise of certain victory in every future circumstance, on one simple condition. It is possible to read this verse and miss the condition of blessing laid before Joshua. God

35

said, *Every place that the sole of your foot shall tread upon*. Notice it was the sole of his "foot," not the sole of his "shoe" or "sandal."

This may seem to be a minor detail, but actually it involves a great basic condition. There are several places in the Bible where men were told to remove their shoes from off their feet, because they were standing upon holy ground. The ground was holy because God was there in a special and unique way. Therefore, when they removed their shoes they were recognizing the presence of God.

This is what is implied in verse 3. If Joshua would humbly and reverently recognize the presence of God and act in relation to that presence, then God promised that he would possess every such place.

In verse 3 the promise is—*every place*. In verse 5 we read, "There shall not a man be able to stand before thee all the days of thy life," so the promise here is for "every day." This makes the twofold promise one of tremendous potential—*every place, every day*. This was how God began "The Book of Joshua." To a man full of fear and frustration came this glorious offer of God.

I Corinthians 10 reminds us that this is for us, this can be our warning to fit us for right action by good instruction. Pause for a moment and consider that this is one of the promises of God that finds its answer in Christ, and realize that what God was saying to Joshua long ago He is saying to you and to me today.

The "Program" God gave to Joshua is found in verse 8. This is a long verse of forty-eight words but every word is packed with powerful instruction from God. It concerns "This book of the Law." This is a reference to Joshua's Bible. Certainly it would be much shorter than ours, but it was to be the center of his daily program for God.

The directions were that Joshua had to *meditate therein day and night*. This called for a special time to be set aside morning and evening during which he could meditate on the Word of God. If we consider that Joshua was probably one of the busiest men who ever lived, this command comes to us with special force.

Many of us are so busy keeping up with our daily program that somehow it becomes increasingly difficult to find time and space for the Word of God. But when we consider that Joshua was busy in the things of God all day long, not in the things of the world, and yet he needed these special times of meditation, then how much more is this true for us.

Notice, also, that God's program was not "reading" the Word of God, but "meditating" therein. Meditation is fast becoming a lost art. The emphasis today is on speed reading whereby the student is able to "devour" an increasing number of words each minute—but this wasn't so for Joshua. Reading is one-way traffic whereby my eyes go to the script and sweep by hurriedly to the end. Meditation is two-way traffic whereby my eyes go to the words and the words return to my conscious area of thought. Psalm 119 uses the word "meditate" in verses 15, 23, 48, 78, 97, 99 and 148. The purpose of meditation is seen in verse 11 of this same Psalm, "Thy word have I hid in my heart, that I might not sin against thee."

Meditation provides food for thought, a background to life, material for good works and weapons with which to attack and resist the world, the flesh and the devil. As a cow chews the cud, thereby extracting additional food value from what was eaten, so the magic of meditation blesses again and again the one who meditates. This was how God made sure that Joshua's soul would be fed so that he could grow and cope with the inrush of the demands of those needy people.

The whole purpose of Joshua 1:8 is seen in the last two phrases, "for then thou shalt make thy way prosperous, and then thou shalt have good success." God's program had a definite purpose in the life of Joshua, just as it would have in your life and mine. There is not a reader who would not desire this same promise of success and prosperity. This is what we long for in all our Christian lives.

But there may be some who say, "Well, I've done all this—I've meditated on God's Word and learned many Scriptures, but it hasn't made my way prosperous nor given me much success!" To such I would say, this verse does not promise success or prosperity to all who meditate in the Bible. This is where so many people can be misguided in their program, and become disillusioned in their practice of it.

The increase of Bible study groups and fellowships is a most blessed thing. Under the hand of God tremendous blessing can come thereby. But Bible study groups are no guarantee of success and prosperity. Attendance at such does not equip one with infallible blessing.

The whole "punch" of verse 8 is found in the center, *that thou mayest observe to do according to all that is written therein.* Obedience is the key to success! Meditation will lead me to the door of blessing, but obedience is the key that opens the door and sends me through.

We must realize that when God was speaking to Joshua He was referring not only to the spiritual blessings to be enjoyed. In a special way this was to be worked out in the practical things of life. Joshua had to apply the knowledge he had gained by meditation to making the choices and decisions in the days ahead.

This is where many of us fail. We somehow assume that the Bible is specifically spiritual and nothing else. I have met many Christians whose spiritual life and church life is acted out in accordance with the Book of Rules, but whose life and behavior in the world around them is conducted under a different pattern. No wonder such people have so little peace and joy and blessing in their hearts. God's program has to be my program for every walk of my life—church, domestic, cultural, business, social and any other area that involves decisions and choices.

Finally, God gave to Joshua the "power" with which this program could be carried through. In verse 6 God had said, *Be strong and of a good courage.* In verse 7 the words were, *Only be thou strong and very courageous.* It is good to learn here that God never calls one of His children to do a task without giving them the means to fulfill that work. If God is calling you to go, or do, or be, for Him, then you can be sure if the call is from God that the power will also come from God.

God was calling on Joshua for an increased demonstration of strength and courage. In your life, at this present moment, there may be conditions and areas that frighten and baffle you, and you feel it is impossible to face up to the situation. Joshua's courage and strength was very low at that moment, then God suddenly called for extra strength and "good courage" and to be "very courageous."

God went further in verse 9 to issue a command. "Have not I commanded thee? Be strong and of a good courage; be not afraid, neither be thou dismayed: for the LORD thy God is with thee whithersoever thou goest." But everything God demanded, God provided. The entire problem was solved in the last ten words of verse 9: *the Lord thy God is with thee whithersoever thou goest.*

Joshua had no strength—but he had to be strong. Joshua had no courage—but he had to be courageous. How was this going to be possible? There was only one answer—Joshua was going to be strong in the strength of another! The One who made the promise of *every place* in verse 3 and *every day* in verse 5 now supplied the power to make the promise a living reality.

The verse we must continue to remember is that with which we began, "For as many as are the promises of God, they all find their Yes (answer) in Him (Christ)" (II Corinthians 1:20, *Amplified Bible*). This, together with the admonition in I Corinthians 10, is how "The Book of Joshua" can lead to "The Book of You."

If you will identify yourself in every way possible, with this man—his age, his fear, his panic, his inability to cope, then, the more you see yourself *in* the story the more blessing you will receive *out* of the story.

The last three verses of this chapter provide a happy sequel to the entire story. Joshua, having been commanded of God in verse 9, then goes out to command the people in verse 10. He claimed the promise, fulfilled the program, exercised the power and stepped out in obedience to the will of God. The last three verses give us the reaction of the people to the action of Joshua, "All that thou commandest us we will do, and withersoever thou sendest us we will go" (verse 16).

His obedience to God was reflected in the obedience of the people. In verse 17 they said, "According as we hearkened unto Moses in all things, so will we hearken unto thee: only the LORD thy God be with thee. The chapter ends with these rousing words from the people, "only be strong and of a good courage." All that God said to Joshua was re-echoed in the hearts of the people. His step of simple obedience had won their hearts and they were prepared to commit their lives into the hands of a man whose life was truly committed to God.

This is how this thrilling "Book of Joshua" begins, this is how "The Book of You" could begin. Joshua began anew, so can you. He had wandered for forty years in the wilderness but he got out—by a "promise" and a "program" and a "power."

It matters not how long you have experienced wandering and a wilderness experience. There can be an end to it all. There can be a new life as a child of God. There can be a new and wonderful "Book of You" if you will also accept the "promise," the "program" and the "power," and realize in all this that, all this is true in Christ.

Thank You Heavenly Father, for the Book of Joshua.

Thank You for this man whose need was so great but who found a full satisfaction in his God.

Father, I would see myself in this story.

I confess my fears, my weaknesses, my utter inability to cope with the pressures of life.

Oh, may I receive this promise for every place and every day—in Christ Jesus.

May I become obedient to Thy Word, day and night, so that I may share Thy success—in Christ Jesus.

May I experience the reality of being strong in the strength of another—even Christ Jesus. Amen.

CHAPTER 4

THE PERIL OF IMMATURITY

IN CHAPTER TWO we considered the church at Corinth. We saw how the Corinthians were addressed as, *the church of God . . . sanctified in Christ Jesus . . . called saints.* But we found that what they were by the grace of God, and how they lived in the power of the flesh, were two different things. We saw their envying and strife and divisions. We were amazed at their sexual looseness, and distressed by their treatment of one another in the law courts. We saw that all this came because they were babes in Christ—they had never gone on to real maturity.

We reflected that this was a challenge to us to examine the quality of our lives. We need to do this still further in the light of the deeper challenge that Paul brought to these people at Corinth.

In I Corinthians 3:9-16 the Holy Spirit reveals a new line of teaching which should make every one of us stop in our tracks and measure up to the peril of continuing to live a life of insipid immaturity. The entire section is concerned with the works done by the Christian.

Beginning with verse 11 we read,

For other foundation can no man lay than that is laid, which is Jesus Christ.

12 Now if any man build upon this foundation gold, silver, precious stones, wood, hay, stubble;

13 Every man's work shall be made manifest: for the day

42

shall declare it, because it shall be revealed by fire; and the
fire shall try every man's work of what sort it is.

14 If any man's work abide which he hath built thereupon, he shall receive a reward.

15 If any man's work shall be burned, he shall suffer loss:
but he himself shall be saved; yet so as by fire.

16 Know ye not that ye are the temple of God, and that
the Spirit of God dwelleth in you?

These are words of tremendous importance and they
become increasingly so when we put them alongside II
Corinthians 5:9-11, words which were written to the
same people,

9 Wherefore we labour, that, whether present or absent,
we may be accepted of him.

10 For we must all appear before the judgment seat of
Christ; that every one may receive the things done in his
body, according to that he hath done, whether it be good or
bad.

11 Knowing therefore the terror of the Lord, we persuade
men; but we are made manifest unto God.

Notice that these Corinthian Christians were being
told to be ready *for the day . . . for the judgment seat of
Christ*. This latter phrase is also to be found in Romans
14:10, so that we have here a threefold witness to a
coming day in the life of every believer.

The Judgment Seat of Christ must not be confused
with the Great White Throne. The only similarity between the two is the fact that the Lord Jesus Christ is
the Judge in each case. We need to see that Revelation
20:12 is specific when it says, "And I saw the dead,
small and great, stand before God." Again in verse 13
we are assured that those who appear before the Great
White Throne are *the dead*.

Everyone who has been born again has ceased to be
numbered among the dead. They have become the
living ones and their names are in the Lamb's Book of
Life. That is why in this same verse 12 we read, "I saw
the dead, small and great, stand before God; and the

books were opened: and another book was opened, which is the book of life: and the dead were judged out of those things which were written in the books, according to their works."

The dead have their names and their deeds recorded in the many books of the dead and they will be judged out of those things which are written in the books. There is no sign or reference whatever to the presence of the living ones on this terrible occasion. The fact that the Book of Life is there is a double check in case any one should claim that a mistake had been made.

We see this in detail in the words of our Lord in Matthew 7:21-23. He indicated that, "Not every one that saith unto me, Lord, Lord, shall enter into the kingdom of heaven." He explained that, "Many will say to me in that day, Lord, Lord, have we not prophesied in thy name? and in thy name have cast out devils? and in thy name done many wonderful works?" These were people seeking to justify themselves on the grounds of what they had done. Then the Lord gave His final and awful answer to all such, "And then will I profess unto them, I never knew you: depart from me, ye that work iniquity."

The one simple test was this: *I never knew you.* How this issues forth into strong relief the words of Christ in John 10:27, 28, "My sheep hear my voice, and I know them, and they follow me: And I give unto them eternal life; and they shall never perish, neither shall any pluck them out of my hand."

Those whom He knows have eternal life. Because they have this quality of life they have been born again. Because they have been born again and have life, their names are in the Lamb's Book of Life. Because their names are in the Book of Life they will never stand before the Great White Throne.

Those whom He knows not are still spiritually dead. They may be church members, holding office and doing many wonderful works. But, as the Lord taught in

Matthew 7, if He knows them not, they have no place in His kingdom.

This should cause every reader to pause and be sure in his own heart that he has been born again—that he has reality and not religion. The need for this double check is so necessary when we hear the Lord Jesus saying, *Many will say to me!*

The Judgment Seat of Christ is therefore quite different from the Great White Throne. The Great White Throne is concerned with eternal judgment. The Judgment Seat of Christ is concerned with rewards, not punishments. This fact needs to be fully understood at the outset.

I Corinthians 3:14 says, "If any man's work abide . . . he shall receive a reward." The next verse goes on to state, "If any man's work shall be burned, he shall suffer loss: but he himself shall be saved; yet so as by fire." The entire purpose of this Judgment Seat is the giving or the withholding of rewards.

Anyone who gets to this Seat is already saved, born again, sure of eternal life and blessing.

This teaching was vitally necessary to the Corinthian church. They were unconcerned about the quality of life they were living. They were satisfied to know they were babes in Christ, saved by the blood of Christ and that they were going to heaven when they died. The Holy Spirit was opening to them the tremendous truth that their lives were going to be examined and tested in a coming day.

This teaching is equally necessary today. We need to be aware of the peril of immaturity. Every one of us needs to be jolted into a conscious and positive realization that he will have to stand before the Lord to give an account of his life.

The phrase, The Judgment Seat of Christ, is a picture word, taken from the customs and behavior of the people of New Testament times. The picture is that of a lord, or a ruler, who has been away from his kingdom, returning and making a critical survey of what each of his servants has done in his absence. Each one would come before him and give an account of what he had done, showing whether his time had been spent profitably in his master's service. The ruler would carefully consider the efforts of each of his servants and, as he evaluated their work, he would give them rewards commensurate with their value.

Some of the servants would receive worthy and honorable rewards, some would receive a nominal gift, while others, because of their laziness or lack of effort, would receive nothing. The entire ceremony was concerned with the giving, or the withholding, of rewards.

This is what our passages teach us concerning our own lives and their value to the Lord Jesus Christ.

Check back in our passages and see how personal this Judgment Seat of Christ is. In I Corinthians 3 there is a constant emphasis on the words *every man* and *any man*. Verses 10, 12, 13 (twice), 14, 15 indicate this truth. II Corinthians 5:10 emphasizes that, "we must all appear before the judgment seat of Christ; that every one may receive."

Notice, too, in I Corinthians 3:9, that "we are laborers together with God" and in II Corinthians 5:9 we read, "Wherefore we labour, that, whether present or absent, we may be accepted of him." The emphasis is on the word "labor." We are not seated in secluded splendor apart from the rush and turmoil of a busy world. We are out in the midst of it, experiencing weariness and exhaustion for the Lord's sake.

The Judgment Seat of Christ is concerned with things that are both personal and practical. The picture we have is of the Lord seated, and each one of us appearing before Him individually. If anyone should wonder how long such a procedure would take, the answer is very simple—time has ceased to be when this event takes place. Time is of no consequence.

If we were to stop and consider that at one specific moment in the economy of God we would each stand before the Lord Jesus, what a difference this would make in our lives. So much of what we are occupied with is just froth and bubble which has absolutely no significance when viewed against the background of the Judgment Seat of Christ.

Consider the deliberate and serious language of Paul in II Corinthians 5:9-11, "Wherefore we labor ... we may be accepted of him ... we must all appear ... knowing therefore the terror of the Lord ... we persuade men." This was the biggest thing in Paul's life. Notice the phrase, *Knowing therefore the terror of the Lord*. This in no way implies that Paul was being scared into serving God. On the contrary, it shows Paul full of a sense of reverence and awe. He was enveloped with a tremendous sense of the greatness of God. He was conscious that he was to be held accountable to this Holy One for his deeds and desires in this life. Paul had an appointment with Christ in eternity at which time he would give an account of his stewardship in this life.

If this same thought could grip us, what stupendous results might be seen in our lives. Everything we thought, or said, or did, would be seen against a new background. We would rearrange our priorities, and our sense of values would be drastically revised. The words of the Lord in Luke 12:15 need to sound again and again in so many of our hearts and lives.

Consider what Christ said, "Take heed, and beware of covetousness: for a man's life consisteth not in the abundance of the things which he possesseth." Let us be absolutely honest and say that in many of our lives we do not, *Take heed or beware*. Abundance of things plays a great part in so many Christian lives today. We line up our philosophy with the way of the world, and gather things and more things. When we do so we imply that this is what life is meant to be in our eyes. Poverty has never been detrimental to the power of the

47

Church, but wealth has often weakened, and destroyed, and diverted, the main thrust of the Christian life.

Paul was gripped with this overruling sense of utter reverence and responsibility. He knew that some day the Lord would go through his life page by page. This would be the divine demonstration of "This Is Your Life." This realization in no way destroyed his appetite for living or his joy in life—it was the overruling pattern by which his life moved on from day to day.

This was what the Holy Spirit was bringing as a challenge to those spiritual babes in Corinth. They needed to beware of the peril of immaturity. They needed to take stock of the quality of living flowing out from their daily experience.

I Corinthians 3:10 tells us that what is under review at the Judgment Seat of Christ is the work that we have done for the Lord. This is not our sin being judged, this is our work being reviewed. Our sin is dealt with through the precious, shed blood of Christ. There is no question here of my sin and my own deliberate failure and shame. Thank God for the forgiveness and cleansing that follows the confession and sorrow.

All of us, in one way or another, are building on the foundation described in verse 11. Some of the works we do may be excellent, some may be satisfactory. With so many of us, we are completely unaware that we are building day by day in thought, word, or deed. We are always witnesses for Christ, but our heedless, careless, selfish lives so often make a witness which is anything but to His glory.

So it is that verse 12 divides the quality of our work into six separate categories—gold, silver, precious stones, wood, hay and stubble. Your Christian life so far will be a mixture of the six components. Notice, here, there is a descending order of values, beginning with the costliness of the pure gold and ending with the empty, spent, uselessness of dry, brittle stubble.

But while there are six different groups there are only

two classes of works—those that remain, and those that are consumed. Verse 13 describes how these six groups are tested—they are tried by fire. Notice that it is the works that are tried by fire, not the Christian.

Gold, silver, and precious stones will remain untouched by the fire, but the wood, hay and stubble will disappear in a cloud of smoke. It is a beautiful thought to consider that gold and silver can withstand the fire because that is how they are produced. They have already passed through the refiner's fire and therefore they are pure. Precious stones are produced in the earth by pressure and intense heat, so they, too, can withstand the testing of the Lord. This gives us a true indication of the quality of the works that please God and which meet with His approval at the Judgment Seat of Christ. They are essentially pure—refined as in gold and silver. They are the result of pressure and testing and fire, and each one had to be dug out of the earth by labor and toil.

This same passage in I Corinthians 3 gives us the two essential standards against which our works are to be judged. Verse 13 says, *the fire shall try every man's work of what sort it is.* Notice that last phrase, *of what sort it is.* This is the standard by which your Christian life will be judged. It is not "how big it is," or "how much it is," but simply *what sort it is.*

Basically, there are two sorts possible, and your work for Christ will be one or the other. When the Lord Jesus was speaking to Nicodemus in John 3:6, He uttered a most profound saying which has unlimited application, "That which is born of the flesh is flesh; and that which is born of the Spirit is spirit." There are two sorts of work possible—that which is born of the flesh and that which is born of the Spirit.

Do not be misled into thinking that the term "flesh" is either a physical reference, denoting only the flesh upon our bones, or that it is a spiritual reference denoting only evil, lust, impurity and godlessness. The term "the flesh" in the Bible means, "all that a man is, without Christ." It may mean evil and sin and impurity. It can also mean all those characteristics of human goodness—graciousness, elegance, and charm. These are also the marks of the flesh. Some people are naturally gracious and tenderhearted, just as others seem to be born to cause trouble.

When a sinner receives Christ as his personal Saviour he is born again. He receives a new quality of life. The Lord Jesus comes to dwell in his heart and life in the person of His Holy Spirit (Revelation 3:20). The sinner began by being only in the flesh, but salvation brings him the indwelling Spirit also. So a Christian has both the flesh and the Spirit—he is a partaker of the divine nature (II Peter 1:4).

When verse 13 of I Corinthians 3 says, *of what sort it is,* this is how there can be two sorts. There can be that which I have done for Christ, that which I have originated, the product of my own fleshly activity. Or there can be that which has come through the outworking of the indwelling Christ.

That which is born of the flesh is flesh, and Romans 8:8 teaches, *they that are in the flesh cannot please God.* The flesh always wants to have its own way, whether bad or good. It is not subject to God, it is an open demonstration of independence put out in defiance of the Lord Himself.

That which is born of the Spirit is what has come in my life as I have yielded and continued to yield my life to Christ. He has been in control. His will has been done through me, so that the works that come as a result are truly the works of the Spirit. These are the works that bring glory to Christ, that fulfill His will and that stand the test of the fire at the Judgment Seat of Christ.

So when verse 13 says, *of what sort it is,* we know now what is implied. There are two sorts—"my sort" and "His sort." "My sort" are the wood, hay and stubble. "His sort" are the gold, silver and precious stones.

There is one other essential standard we need to see in I Corinthians 3. Verse 10 says, "But let every man take heed how he buildeth thereupon." In verse 13 it was *what sort it is,* now in verse 10 it is *how he builds.* Notice that this is simply "how" you do the work, it is not "how much" or "how big," but simply the manner in which you set about your work for Christ.

If we think about this word "how" it becomes quite an important challenge. I can serve the Lord and be involved in my church or my group simply because I am expected to do this. If I did not join in, then hints would be given, criticisms implied, and questions asked, so I do it just because of others.

I can also serve the Lord in order to draw attention to myself. I get myself in the limelight and win for myself a good name, so I'm happy to do it to win praise.

I can also serve as a means of promoting myself, my job, my family. It will be good for business and people will be able to learn about me and what I can do.

There are endless reasons for "how" we do our work for Christ, but only a few are going to count at the Judgment Seat of Christ. First and foremost it should be out of deep responsive love to Christ. How do I do it? Willingly, gladly, with all my heart, with no reserve or holding back.

The "how" and the "what sort it is" will decide whether we hear those wonderful words, "Well done, thou good and faithful servant: thou hast been faithful over a few things ... enter thou into the joy of thy lord" (Matthew 25:21, 23).

As to what the rewards are, we have no real indication. It says in I Corinthians 3:14, *he shall receive a reward.* Revelation 22:12—the last chapter in the Bible —states, "And, behold, I come quickly; and my reward is with me, to give every man according as his work shall be." Therefore we see a definite teaching of rewards for work done. Many of us would say that we want no reward, that just to be with Jesus will be our blessing and our greatest joy. This is good and a most commendable attitude, but the reward is connected with the Judgment Seat, and this will be a place of real heart searching. Some will lose their reward, whatever that may be.

Many of us may feel that this is something we can quietly leave until we get to glory, but Paul didn't agree with this. He had that deep earnestness of desire that filled his whole being—*For me to live is Christ!* He challenged the heedless, careless Corinthians who were content to be babes in Christ.

Remember that I Corinthians is also written to us (see 1:2). This is something we have to face and something on which we have to act and react. The peril of immaturity in your life could blight your witness, paralyze your work and send you to the Judgment Seat with emptiness and shame.

> Only one life,
> 'Twill soon be past.
> Only what's done for Christ
> Will last.

A PRAYER FOR MEDITATION

Father, as I search my heart and life I see the empty wasted days, weeks, months and years.

Forgive me that I have been content to be spiritually immature.

I have never thought of "what sort it is," or "how" my life has progressed in relationship to the Judgment Seat of Christ. So much has been "my sort" carelessly and heedlessly done.

Teach me, good Lord, to serve Thee as Thou deservest—to give and not to count the cost.

To fight and not to heed the wounds.

To toil and not to seek for rest.

To labor and not to ask for any reward, save that of knowing that I do Thy will. In Jesus' name do I pray. Amen.

CHAPTER 5

JOSHUA—
THE ONE CONDITION OF ALL BLESSING

As our book continues we will see, more clearly, the great similarity there is between the teaching in the New Testament concerning the need for going on to maturity, and the progressive experiences set forth in the life of Joshua. Each one is complementary to the other.

In chapter two we considered our great need as set forth in the Corinthian and Hebrew epistles. In chapter three we discussed how the need in Joshua's life was going to be met by God. Chapter four emphasized the need for a determined response to God. Now this chapter, dealing with Joshua's life once more, is going to show us how that determined response can be accomplished.

In chapter three we noticed that God gave Joshua a "promise," a "program," and a "power." The entire Book of Joshua was to be the record of that man's response to this threefold approach from God.

Let us pick up the story once more as we find it in Joshua 1:3, "Every place that the sole of your foot shall tread upon, that have I given unto you, as I said unto Moses." This was part of the twofold promise of God— every place—every day.

In this way God began to deal with Joshua. The words, *Every place that the sole of your foot shall tread upon,* mark the commencement of God's reasoning with him. Everything else that God had to say was consequent upon this initial approach. In one sense everything else that God had for Joshua was dependent upon his response to this first great condition.

We have already considered the significance of the words, *The sole of your foot.* This was not the sole of his shoe or his sandal, but his bare foot placed on the ground. In doing this Joshua would demonstrate the presence of God. He would show that he was standing on holy ground. And it was this acceptance of God's presence which was to be the guarantee of all future victory.

If we look back to Exodus 3 we see the same detail being worked out in the life of Moses. Verse 1 tells us that Moses was at *the backside of the desert* when God came into his life. What a potent phrase this is. He was not just in the desert, he was in the backside of the desert—the ultimate in failure and barrenness!

Exodus 7:7 tells us that Moses was eighty years old when this happened. He had already lived forty years in the glamor and glory of Egypt as the son of Pharaoh's daughter. Acts 7:22 says, "Moses was learned in all the wisdom of the Egyptians, and was mighty in words and deeds." This is a tremendous statement, because the Egyptians possessed unique qualities of wisdom covering many fields of knowledge, and yet Moses was learned in *all* this wisdom. In our language today we would say that he had several Ph.D. degrees. He was also *mighty in words and deeds.* Not only was he supremely learned, but he also had a tremendous capacity for communicating his knowledge. He was a man of action.

Such a combination of gifts and talents marks Moses as one of the greatest men of all ages. This was proved to be so in his later exploits as the leader of God's people.

But, Exodus 3 begins with this amazing man in the backside of the desert. All his wisdom, his words and his works were devoted to shepherding a flock of sheep or goats. What an utter waste of time and ability! Acts 7:30 tells us that he did this work for forty years. For forty years he was a nobleman, then for forty years he was a nobody. After that God spoke to him.

Exodus 3:2 goes on to describe the incident of the burning bush. Notice Moses' first words, "I will now turn aside, and see." God made the approach but Moses had to turn aside and see. Everything began when Moses turned aside—what a significant challenge to us.

Verse 4 tells of God's response when Moses did turn aside, "God called unto him out of the midst of the bush." God called his name twice and Moses replied, *Here am I.*

Then comes the importance of verse 5. God said, "Draw not nigh hither: put off thy shoes from off thy feet, for the place whereon thou standest is holy ground." As it was with Joshua, so it was with Moses. God's first approach was the challenge to recognize the presence of deity by standing with the sole of the foot on bare ground.

All that happened from then on in the life of Moses came because he recognized the presence of a Holy God in his life. This is something we need to experience in our own hearts and lives. Some of us may be, today, *in the backside of the desert,* wasting our potential in lonely areas. What we need is this face to face confrontation with God, with the reality of a holy God, so that our immediate response is to recognize His holiness by standing in the presence of deity.

An interesting thought here is that shoes were worn by free men but slaves walked barefooted. Therefore, when a man removed his shoes in the presence of God he was resigning his freedom and recognizing himself as a slave in God's sight. *Not my will, but Thine be done.*

We can now go on to see Joshua's response to the promise of God. In Joshua 3 are recorded the preparations that Joshua made to cross the river Jordan into the land of Canaan. So far Joshua had done no miracle, nor had there been any demonstration of God's authority vested in him. But in verse 7 we read, "The LORD said unto Joshua, This day will I begin to magnify thee in the sight of all Israel, that they may know that, as I was with Moses, so I will be with thee."

Joshua was going to magnify God and God was going to magnify Joshua.

Then in verse 8 God told Joshua to command the priests that bore the ark saying, "When ye are come to the brink of the water of Jordan, ye shall stand still in Jordan." Here was a tremendous challenge of faith. Verse 15 tells us that the Jordan was overflowing all its banks, so that it was not a tiny trickle but a full-flowing river, capable of damage and destruction. Yet Joshua had to proclaim by faith that when the priests came to the water's edge they would be able to *stand still in Jordan.*

Consider Joshua making the utterly impossible announcement that this thing would happen. He had no rod of Moses that parted the Red Sea, nor had he a cloak of Elijah to separate the waters. All he had was a promise from God, *Every place that the sole of your foot shall tread upon, that have I given unto you.* The way to victory was the recognition of deity!

See now what happened as recorded in verse 13, "And it shall come to pass, as soon as the feet of the priests that bear the ark of the LORD, the Lord of all the earth, shall rest in the waters of Jordan, that the waters of Jordan shall be cut off from the waters that come down from above; and they shall stand upon an heap." These are the words spoken by Joshua to the people. Joshua was taking this great step of faith, but notice what he said, *as soon as the feet of the priests.* He was going to claim the promise of God.

Verse 15 describes what happened next. It says, "The feet of the priests that bore the ark were dipped in

57

the brim of water," and the river parted so that they were able to *stand still in Jordan.*

Joshua 4:3 tells of Joshua commanding that twelve memorial stones be taken out of Jordan, "out of the place where the priests' feet stood firm." In verse 9 he places twelve more stones "in the midst of Jordan, in the place where the feet of the priests stood."

Verse 18 tells how this miraculous crossing was ended. It states specifically that when *the soles of the priests' feet were lifted up unto the dry land,* the Jordan flowed in full force once more.

Thus it was that Joshua was magnified in the presence of all the people, but only because he had the people standing with bare feet. A simple act of obedience brought the blessing he so much needed.

You will remember that I Corinthians 10 told us to look at these stories, and see ourselves in the incidents recorded—to see if there is a lesson that we need to learn, or a warning we need to take.

Here then is one definite lesson every one of us must learn—so simple yet so vital—as I recognize the presence of God, so I experience the power of God.

But Joshua had to learn not only to "recognize the presence of God," but he also had to discover the tremendous importance of "practicing the presence of God." This is shown in a story which begins in Joshua 5.

In chapter 5 the people are safely across the Jordan. They have established themselves in the Promised Land, and Joshua is now planning to move on to the next item on their schedule—the capture and destruction of the city of Jericho.

In verse 13 we have a picture of Joshua, by himself, standing and viewing the city of Jericho from a distance. He had probably seen this city once before, forty years ago when he, along with Caleb and the other spies, had made a reconnaissance of the land of Canaan. Of those who had seen Jericho before, only

Joshua and Caleb remained alive. None of the children of Israel had ever seen a walled city—they knew nothing but life in the wilderness. Therefore Joshua would be viewing this strong strategic city. This was to be no easy task, for Jericho was built especially strong to withstand the attacks of a well-organized army.

As Joshua looked and pondered the entire situation he was suddenly aware of another man standing not too far away. This other man was armed and he stood with a drawn sword in his hand. Obviously the man was prepared to fight—he was no man of peace.

Joshua's response was immediate. He approached the armed stranger, probably with his own sword drawn in case of sudden attack. He challenged the newcomer, "Art thou for us, or for our adversaries?" (5:13). Here was no wasting of words. Joshua didn't trouble to ask for the man's name. All he wanted to know was, "Whose side are you on—our side or their side?"

There was a slight pause, and then the unknown stranger spoke. He first answered Joshua's question with one word "Neither!"—"I am not here to take sides." Then he told Joshua who he was, "as captain of the host of the LORD am I now come" (verse 14). This One had not come to take sides, He had come to take over. He was to be in charge of the whole of "Operation Jericho." He had command of the entire army of God and, as such, was in complete control of the situation.

Joshua's response was immediate. He fell on his face to the earth. He worshiped this Holy One and said, "What saith my Lord unto his servant?" He quickly handed over the entire problem to the Holy One, called Him Lord, and asked for orders as a servant would do.

Notice in verse 15 the one command that Joshua received, "And the captain of the LORD's host said unto Joshua, Loose thy shoe from off thy foot; for the place whereon thou standest is holy. And Joshua did so." There was only one thing needed from Joshua—not only to recognize the presence of God, but also to practice the presence of God.

Joshua had stood there alone, in his own strength, facing a problem he could never have solved. All the while the answer was his in the promise of God found in chapter 1, *Every place that the sole of your foot shall tread upon, that have I given unto you.* Knowing the promise was one thing, but practicing that promise was another.

So it was that here again God taught Joshua the reality of the promises of God. Joshua actually saw, for the first and last time, the Prince of the army of God. What he had heard with his ears he saw now with his own eyes. God's promises came true in a Person.

This Person could be none other than the Lord Jesus Christ. He was Deity and He demanded worship, yet He stood before Joshua in the body of a man. What an amazing thought that Joshua, in his day, was going to be able to say—as Paul wrote later—"I can do all things through Christ which strengtheneth me" (Philippians 4:13).

God had given Joshua a "promise," a "program" and a "power." The power we saw in Joshua 1:9, *the Lord thy God is with thee whithersoever thou goest.* Now the presence of the Prince of God was the answer to the power he needed. Both the promise and the power came true in the Person of Christ.

I Corinthians 10 asks—Is there any thing you can learn from this? Do you have a Jericho next on your schedule? Is there some problem, some situation, which is continuing to baffle you? Why don't you not only recognize the presence of God in Christ but also practice His presence, moment by moment. He has said, "I will never leave thee, nor forsake thee" (Hebrews 13:5).

It is interesting here, for a moment, to consider the Lord Jesus as the Captain or Prince of the army of God. In Matthew 26:51-53, Peter stood in the Garden of Gethsemane with a sword drawn in his hand. He was prepared to defend the Son of God! But Jesus said, "Thinkest thou that I cannot now pray to my Father, and he shall presently give me more than twelve legions of angels?" (verse 53). A legion was 6,000 men, so that the Lord Jesus was stating that more than 72,000 angels were ready to move at His request. Still He did not call for help. Once again He was in control of the entire situation.

We see Joshua's twofold truth, "recognizing the presence of God" and "practicing the presence of God," in Paul's beautiful prayer in Ephesians 3:14-19,

> 14 For this cause I bow my knees unto the Father of our Lord Jesus Christ,
> 15 Of whom the whole family in heaven and earth is named,
> 16 That he would grant you, according to the riches of his glory, to be strengthened with might by his Spirit in the inner man;
> 17 That Christ may dwell in your hearts by faith . . .
> 19 . . . that ye might be filled with all the fulness of God.

This is a tremendous passage. It is not only a wonderful prayer of faith, but also a clear and definite statement of truth set forth in logical sequence.

To understand the sequence better we need to turn to I Thessalonians 5:23 and see there another prayer of Paul which again reveals glorious truth, "And the very God of peace sanctify you wholly; and I pray God your whole spirit and soul and body be preserved blameless unto the coming of our Lord Jesus Christ."

Notice the spelling of the word "wholly." Some people say the word and think it is spelled "holy." It is not "sanctified holy," but *sanctified wholly*. In other words, the power of the Spirit of God is to be seen in every part of my life.

This verse teaches that there are three parts to my humanity. In Genesis 1:26 God had said, "Let us make man in our image, after our likeness." This does not

61

imply that man was going to look like God for *God is a Spirit*, but that man in his humanity in some way was to be like God in His deity. Notice that God said, *Let us*—this was the voice of the Triune God, the Holy Trinity: Father, Son and Holy Spirit. What God was in His essential being—a Trinity—man was going to be in his essential being.

Thus it is we have the trinity of man—spirit, soul and body. Man is not just a body and a soul—that is, a physical body plus a human personality—but spirit, soul and body (trichotomy).

The soul of man in the Bible is often called the heart of man—what we would today call his personality. People remember us, not so much because of our body —our beauty or lack of beauty—but because of the impact of our human personality.

This is a tremendous blessing, because many of us are not initially physically attractive. We all have our significant areas of physical deficiency! But a gracious, loving personality can completely overshadow and hide the physical failures.

The soul of man—or the heart of man—or the personality—is itself a trinity. Modern psychology and the Bible agree in defining three areas in the personality. The names used for the areas may differ, but the significance is the same. These areas are—the emotions— the mind, or intellect—the will.

We can find Scriptures to show each of these areas.

The emotions are clearly indicated in Matthew 15:19 where the Lord Jesus said, "For out of the heart proceed evil thoughts, murders, adulteries, fornications, thefts, false witness, blasphemies." This is the display of intense emotional disturbance.

Again in Luke 1:51 we read, "he hath scattered the proud in the imagination of their hearts." This is the emotional seat of all pride and vanity.

In John 14:1 the Lord Jesus said, "Let not your

heart be troubled." The emotion of fear is evident in the human heart.

The fact that the mind is also a part of the human heart is seen clearly in Matthew 9:4 where we read, "And Jesus knowing their thoughts said, Wherefore think ye evil in your hearts?"

Again in Mark 2:8 we read, "Immediately . . . Jesus . . . said unto them, Why reason ye these things in your heart?" The heart was thus the place where the mind and the intellect could function.

In Daniel 1:8 we read these words, "But Daniel purposed in his heart." He was determined, his will was in evidence. Thus we can see from the Bible the clear threefold teaching concerning the soul, or heart, or personality of man.

It was this threefold concept of man that Paul was concerned with in his prayer, already referred to, in Ephesians 3. Paul was praying for a total involvement of the whole man.

We can understand Paul's sequence of thought if we get a simple visual aid in our mind. Consider a circle—an inner circle. Then, see this inner circle surrounded by another circle—thus giving two concentric circles. Then, put one more circle around that picture and you have something like a target as used in archery—an inner circle plus two more concentric circles.

The inner circle we can call the spirit. The circle surrounding that we can call the soul—or personality. The outer circle then becomes, of course, the body.

We are now in a position to line up the two truths that Joshua learned with the great prayer that Paul prayed.

Joshua had to learn, first, to "recognize the presence of God"—then, to keep on "practicing the presence of God."

Paul prayed first in Ephesians 3:16 that they might be "strengthened with might by his Spirit in the inner man." The inner man is that inner circle—the human spirit. Paul thus wanted the Ephesians to realize first of all that becoming a Christian was not just having their sins forgiven, but also having a real, conscious sense of the Spirit in their human spirits.

This is seen again in Romans 8:16 where Paul says, "The Spirit himself beareth witness with our spirit, that we are the children of God." I become a child of my parents when I am born the first time. I become a child of God when I am born again. This is *how* I am born again—by the Spirit Himself coming to dwell in my human spirit. This is also *where* I am born again, and *when* I am born again.

Remember, the Lord Jesus said in John 3:3, "Except a man be born again, he cannot see the kingdom of God." If I have not received the Spirit, then I am not born again, I am not a child of God.

Romans 8:9 says, "But ye are not in the flesh, but in the Spirit, if so be that the Spirit of God dwell in you. Now if any man have not the Spirit of Christ, he is none of his." Notice the tremendous significance of this verse—the Holy Spirit is the Spirit of Christ. The Lord Jesus dwells within us in the presence of His Spirit. If He is not there, then I am not a Christian.

So Paul's first request was that these Christians might *be strengthened with might by his Spirit in the inner man—the human spirit*. As with Joshua, so they were to recognize the presence of God.

This is something so many Christians have never truly realized by conscious personal application. They know they have been saved by the blood of Christ. They know, like the Israelites, they have been redeemed from Egypt—from the bondage of sin: that their sins are forgiven by the death of Christ.

What they fail to realize is this very thing for which Paul prayed, that, because they were saved, they might be strengthened with might by His Spirit in their human spirit.

God's salvation is not only Christ *for* me on the

cross, but Christ *in* me through His Spirit. And the fact of Christ *in* me is the realization of the presence of God.

The presence of Christ brings the power of Christ. That is why Paul prayed *strengthened with might*. The Greek word which is translated "might" is *dunamis*. This word is expressive of intense power. It is from this word that the word dynamite was coined—an explosive and eruptive force.

In other words, when I become a Christian, the Lord Jesus comes to dwell in my inner man, my human spirit, and because He is there I have within me the explosive, eruptive power of God.

When I realize this, then I recognize the presence of God. But Joshua also had to practice the presence of God. For me this means the application of this indwelling power day by day in my human life.

Paul indicated this when he went on to pray in Ephesians 3:17, "That Christ may dwell in your hearts by faith." To understand this more clearly, think once again of those three concentric circles. First was the inner one—the human spirit. Second was the middle one—the heart or the human personality.

Recognizing the presence of God is realizing that the Lord Jesus dwells in my inner man—practicing His presence is allowing Christ to move into the area of my human personality.

Notice the words, "allowing Christ." This is the test of "practicing the presence of Christ." There are many Christians who have been born again, but who are content to rest on the knowledge of sins forgiven and a home in heaven. They choose to run their own lives their own way. Their emotions, minds and wills are entirely at their own disposal. What they want, or what they say, is the experience of their daily life.

Paul's prayer becomes fulfilled when I, first of all, recognize that the Lord Jesus dwells within my human spirit. Then, when I open my personality to Christ, *He is able to dwell in my heart by faith.* My Lord Jesus moves out of the inner circle into the middle circle of my personality.

This means that He moves into the area of my emotions, my mind or intellect, and my will. The words *dwell in your heart* are more clearly defined in the *Amplified Bible,* "May Christ through your faith [actually] dwell—settle down, abide, make His permanent home—in your hearts!"

This is not a temporary visit but a permanent residency. It is not calling in Christ, as one would call in a doctor to make a house visit. The doctor comes, diagnoses and departs, and in one sense we hope we will never need him again. Conversely, if things go wrong, we can always call him in once more.

This is not the way to practice the presence of Christ. I practice His presence when I invite Him to *settle down, abide, make His permanent home.* This He will do in every area of my personality. It will be Christ dwelling in my emotions, Christ dwelling in my mind, and Christ dwelling in my will.

Remember, also, that when Christ comes in, the power comes in. He comes in to control. This is what it means to be filled with the Spirit. This is not me having more of the Spirit, but the Spirit having more of me. Being filled with the Spirit is being controlled by the Spirit.

Being filled with the Spirit will not result in my going into a wild ecstatic orbit of spiritual aberration. As I am filled, so I will be controlled and my new Christian experience will be the demonstration of the life of Christ through my emotions, my mind and my will.

One immediate result will be the explosive and eruptive power of Christ within the confines of my personality. Notice how the Lord Jesus can often change a human personality—by controlling it and by cleansing it—as He did the Temple.

Not only will the presence of Christ in my human

personality be controlling and cleansing, but it will also be costly. This is why so many of us are not prepared to practice the presence of Christ day by day. It becomes too costly and probably too embarrassing.

It is much easier to recognize the presence of Christ and then run things my own way. I seem to be getting the best of both worlds. In truth, I am experiencing the poverty of two situations.

Paul continued his prayer by adding, in verse 19, "that ye might be filled with all the fulness of God." If we think once more of our three concentric circles this final request is really the extension of the entire outreach of Christ. Beginning in my spirit, the fullness of God will control my human personality, and my own body will be the area where the impact is seen in the world around.

This is clearly set forth in II Corinthians 4:10, 11, where Paul states his own desire, "that the life also of Jesus might be made manifest in our body . . . that the life also of Jesus might be made manifest in our mortal flesh."

This is the most practical application of truth we can ever meet. This is when my faith gets to my fingers and my truth to my toes. This is what the world is waiting to see—not the indwelling Christ—but the outworking of the indwelling Christ, through me. This is the practice of the presence of Christ.

One natural reaction to this teaching of Paul is the thought that, though it may be wonderful in theory, it is impossible to carry through. Humanly speaking this is true, but Paul gives the secret of success in Ephesians 3:20, "Now, unto him that is able to do exceeding abundantly above all that we ask or think, according to the power that worketh in us."

Not only can this be true, but it will become abundantly true, *above all that we ask or think*. It comes true through the power that worketh in us. The power that comes within the inner man is the same power that will be seen through the outer man, but only inasmuch as we are prepared to yield our personalities to the complete control of Christ.

This chapter is called "The One Condition of All Blessing," and this is it. As it was with Joshua, so it is with us. First, we must recognize the presence of Christ, then practice that presence—just living as if it were true—day by day.

A Prayer for Meditation

Heavenly Father, this is a tremendous challenge to my soul.

Thank You that my sins are forgiven—this is so wonderful to me.

Thank You for the indwelling Christ—not only Christ FOR me, but also Christ IN me.

Give me a quiet willingness to cooperate and yield my entire being to You, so that the Lord Jesus can make His permanent home in my redeemed personality.

May the results be that I am more Christlike— because more of me is open to His explosive power. This I pray in the name of my Saviour. Amen.

CHAPTER 6

THE PLAN FOR MATURITY—FOR ME

THERE IS AN OLD SAYING which goes, "Some people eat to live—while others live to eat." In one sense this divides the world into two camps these days—those who go to bed hungry and those who retire, full and sufficed.

But one of the problems of our modern civilization—especially here in America—is that not all the food we eat is food. It may fill and fatten, but it does not all nourish. Thus it is that there has grown up in America the great vitamin industry.

Rightly or wrongly, this is an attempt to give to people the opportunity to make modern food nourishing. Food research scientists have made many wonderful discoveries in the areas of food deficiencies. The results of their studies are seen in the many colored multi-shaped pills which bear intriguing names and which carry amazing promises of blessing to come.

There is no doubt that many people today owe their health and strength—even their very lives—to the work of the vitamin scientists.

Now what is true in the world of physical food is equally true in the realm of spiritual food. As not all physical food is nourishing, so not all spiritual food is nourishing. It may fill and fatten, but it does not bring that excellency of well-being to the blood stream.

There needs to be, in the spiritual food I eat, that unique quality of nourishment that enriches my spiritual blood stream, that puts a sparkle into my spiritual eyes and adds real strength to my spiritual muscles.

The plan for Christian maturity involves the daily absorption of spiritual vitamins. There must be a daily intake so that my spiritual strength is renewed and revitalized.

Maturity is growth in action, and if I am to grow I need a definite vitamin content to my diet—whether it is physical or spiritual growth.

Vitamins, too, are essential to withstand disease and the attacks of germs and viruses. This is true on the physical and spiritual level. There are many Christians who are becoming sick these days—spiritually sick—with diseases and infections brought by germs and viruses. If they had the correct spiritual vitamins in their blood stream they would be able to resist and repel such intrusions.

Deficiency in spiritual vitamins is the cause of much of the sickness in the Church today. So, in this chapter, we will consider the plan for Christian maturity which is based on a simple knowledge of spiritual vitamins.

To make the study easy and understandable we will take the seven separate letters in the word "vitamin" and use each letter to introduce an essential truth, thought or concept, which *must* be in our spiritual blood stream if we are to grow to maturity. The very succession of the letters will bring also a logical progression of truth and teaching.

In this chapter we will consider the four letters V-I-T-A. This will give us teaching on "The Plan for Maturity—*For* Me." In a later chapter we will consider the three letters M-I-N. In that chapter we will consider teaching on, "The Plan for Maturity—*Through* Me."

VICTORY

Our first vitamin then begins with the letter V. There must be a daily realization of the spiritual vitamin of

"Victory" in my life. This is where I begin. The presence, or absence, of victory in my life will color the whole of my daily living. Everything I think, or say, or do, will demonstrate to the world the measure of my victory, or the reality of my defeat.

There can be no peace, until there is victory. This is true in every sphere of human experience. Compromise may prevent war, but it will never produce peace. There has to be the reality of victory before there can be the release of peace.

It is this way in the Christian life. There are many Christians today whose lives are characterized by an absence of peace. They live in a world of trouble, toil and turmoil. They long for peace, they pray for peace, they may even agonize for peace, but they fail to grasp the simple truth that there can be no peace until there is victory.

Let us pursue this thought several stages further by searching in the Word of God.

1. *The Christian faith begins with victory.* In Philippians 2:5-11 we have the complete story of the work of the Lord Jesus Christ. It begins with the poverty of Bethlehem, but it ends with the exaltation of the Lord. He has already been exalted. He already has "a name which is above every name: that at the name of Jesus every knee should bow . . . And that every tongue should confess that Jesus Christ is Lord, to the glory of God the Father."

The whole of my faith is based upon the glorious victory of Christ. Colossians 1:20 says, "having made peace through the blood of his cross." Because the peace has been made, we know the victory has been won.

2. *God's salvation is victory.* Psalm 98:1, 2 has a rich truth to tell, "O sing unto the LORD a new song; for he hath done marvellous things: his right hand, and his holy arm, hath gotten him the victory.

"The LORD hath made known his salvation: his

righteousness hath he openly shewed in the sight of the heathen."

We learned in chapter 1 that all the prophecies of God were fulfilled in the Lord Jesus, and that all the promises of God are true in Him (see II Corinthians 1:20), "For all the promises of God in him are yea, and in him Amen."

See both these truths illustrated in this Psalm. God has made known His salvation—and His salvation is victory—through Christ.

3. *God's victory is to be shared.* I Chronicles 29:11, 12 records David's great words of praise and prayer to Almighty God. Some of the richest conceptions of truth and worship are seen here. "Thine, O LORD, is the greatness, and the power, and the glory, and the victory . . . Both riches and honour come of thee . . . and in thine hand it is to make great, and to give strength unto all."

We see here that this great victory of God is to be shared. It can be known in terms of riches and honor. It can be experienced in greatness and strength—to all.

4. *Victory is a gift to be received.* I Corinthians 15:57 contains one of the greatest encouragements in the Bible, "But thanks be to God, which giveth us the victory through our Lord Jesus Christ."

There may be some who are reading these words with avid interest, because this is what you are seeking —victory over sin—over temptation—over sorrow— fear—anxiety—loneliness—and a thousand other things.

This is what you are working at—seeking, reading, praying, struggling—hoping that some day you will win the victory over this enemy in your life.

Let me give you one amazing word of encouragement—you will never, never win the victory. It matters not how hard you struggle in "blood, toil, tears and sweat," you will never win the victory. Never, because victory is not something you win, it is something you receive! *Thanks be to God, which giveth us the victory.*

All that God has for us, in every area, comes as a gift. "God so loved the world, that he gave his only begotten Son" (John 3:16). "The gift of God is eternal life through Jesus Christ our Lord" (Romans 6:23). "Every good gift and every perfect gift is from above, and cometh down from the Father of lights" (James 1:17). So it is with the experience of victory—it is a gift from God.

The complementary act to giving is not asking, but receiving. I don't ask for a gift that is being offered to me—I take it, and say thank you. I don't earn it or achieve it, nor am I worthy of the gift of God. I simply come with my need and take what is offered.

Just as I came to the cross and accepted Jesus as my Saviour, so I come to the Christ and accept Him as my Victory. I am saved by faith, I walk by faith—even so I have victory by faith.

I don't have to understand it nor be able to explain it—I simply take the victory that God offers in the person of the Lord Jesus Christ.

He dwells in my heart and life through His Holy Spirit. I accept this fact, and on the basis of His presence with me, I accept all the implications of His presence—most of all, His victory lived out through my yielded life.

5. *This is the victory.* I John 5:4 makes this possible to us today, "this is the victory that overcometh the world, even our faith." This is the victory . . . even our faith.

Faith is spelled out F-A-I-T-H. This can be developed as—**F**orsaking **A**ll **I** **T**ake **H**im. This is what faith really is—turning my back on all my failure and taking "all that He is, for all that I need."

At the cross I needed a Saviour from sin, so I turned from my sin and took Christ as my Saviour—taking that which God so freely gave.

Now in the crisis of daily living, I need victory over

those things and experiences that drag me down or turn me aside. The same faith I used at the cross I now use in the crisis. I turn from my petty struggles of failure and I take "all that He is, for all that I need." I take Him as my victory. I commit to my Lord the issues of the problem. I relate to Him the entire situation. Then, with my life fully yielded to Him I go forward in faith, believing that "God is able to make all grace abound toward you; that ye, always having all sufficiency in all things, may abound to every good work" (II Corinthians 9:8).

This then is the vitamin of victory. I need it every day if my life is to count for God and Christ.

I need it and I can experience it. The entire question is—will I take what God offers? There is no alternative to Christ.

INDWELLING HOLY SPIRIT

The first essential vitamin is the reality of victory in my life. This is made possible by the second essential vitamin, an assurance of the indwelling Holy Spirit. Observe that it is the indwelling Spirit who guarantees my victory.

It is not enough to know about the Holy Spirit or to believe in Him—there must be the conscious experience of the indwelling Spirit.

The Holy Spirit dwells within our hearts and lives to represent all that the Lord Jesus Christ is. The Lord said in John 14:26, "But the Comforter (Counselor, Helper, Intercessor, Advocate, Strengthener, Standby), the Holy Spirit, Whom the Father will send in My name [in My place, to represent Me and act on My behalf] He will teach you all things. And He will cause you to recall—will remind you of, bring to your remembrance—everything I have told you" (*Amplified Bible*). His work is to glorify Christ in and through the life of the believer.

74

I Corinthians 2:9 has a wonderful word for us in this respect, "Eye hath not seen, nor ear heard, neither hath entered into the heart of man, the things which God hath prepared for them that love him."

This is so often used as a means of encouraging Christians to endure present trouble so that all these blessings may be theirs when they get to heaven. But how wrong is such an application. The next verse gives us the true interpretation, "But God hath revealed them unto us by his Spirit."

These blessings are for us now, as we allow the indwelling Holy Spirit to control our lives. We can enjoy heaven on the way to heaven—through the same Spirit.

Verse 12 in the same context says, "Now we have received, not the spirit of the world, but the Spirit which is of God; that we might know the things that are freely given to us of God." Observe the impact of truth—*we have received . . . that we might know.*

In chapter 2 of this book we saw the intriguing phrase in Hebrews 6:9, *things that accompany salvation.* The Hebrew Christians had a salvation which had made them babes in Christ, but which had left them dull of hearing and dull of doing. They were short of the *things that accompany salvation.*

What they needed was a conscious sense of the indwelling Holy Spirit, so controlling in their daily lives that they might know the things that were freely given to them of God.

The things freely given were those that could accompany their salvation, that would, in turn, deal with the dullness in their hearing and doing.

In Hebrews 3:12, 14 the writer is still addressing "the holy brethren, partakers of the heavenly calling." He says, "Take heed, brethren, lest there be in any of you an evil heart of unbelief, in departing from the living God. . . . For we are made partakers of Christ, if we hold the beginning of our confidence steadfast unto the end."

He is reminding them of the tremendous potential there is in Christ, if we will only continue in steadfast confidence. It is not only Christ for me on the cross, but the outworking of the indwelling Holy Spirit of Christ in my life day by day.

THANKFULNESS

One of the evidences of our deteriorating society is the growing abandonment of the use of good manners. It is sad to see pleasant, kindly and comforting words and ways being discarded in the desire to be "with it." They cost so little, yet they pay such high dividends and bring unknown rewards to all who use them.

One of these simple customs is the demonstration of an appreciative attitude in saying "thank you."

This is important in the social world around us, but it is much more important in our relationship to our Heavenly Father.

The third great spiritual vitamin essential to a robust and effective Christian life is this continual attitude of thankfulness toward God. A deficiency in this area is clearly seen in a lack of joyous living.

Thankfulness, in a sense, is the button which, when pressed, releases the indwelling Holy Spirit who, in turn brings the victory and the blessing.

I Thessalonians 5:16-18 has significant words to say in this respect. "Rejoice evermore. Pray without ceasing. In every thing give thanks: for this is the will of God in Christ Jesus concerning you."

I am often asked questions concerning the will of God—"How can I know the will of God?"—"What is the will of God for me?" I would say to all who ask that there is a twofold aspect of the will of God. There is the general will of God—this applies to all believers. Then there is the specific will of God—this applies to the individual believer.

There is not much point in pursuing the specific will

of God for my life until I have lined up my daily living against the general will of God.

The general will of God is seen in verse 18 of this passage, "In every thing give thanks: for this is the will of God in Christ Jesus concerning you." Does this mean that I have to thank God for everything, for the times when things go wrong and when trouble and disaster flood my life? It hardly seems sensible to thank God for the disasters and tragedies of life.

Notice the preposition at the beginning of this verse. It is not *for* everything but *in* everything. I don't thank God *for* the tragedy, I thank God *in* the tragedy. I thank Him, in the situation, that I have the means to handle the problem, the tragedy, or whatever it may be.

This is where the third vitamin follows so perfectly after the second.

We have just considered the tremendous basic fact that, because I am a born-again believer, the Lord Jesus dwells within my heart and life through the indwelling Holy Spirit. He is there always and in all ways.

Consider the *Amplified Bible* translation of Hebrews 13:5, "for He (God) Himself has said, I will not in any way fail you *nor* give you up *nor* leave you without support. [I will] not, [I will] not, [I will] not in any degree leave you helpless, *nor* forsake *nor* let [you] down, [relax My hold on you].—Assuredly not!"

This is what we are promised. It is the simple acceptance of this promise that fills our hearts with a quiet confidence.

When my daily life is lived against the background of such blessing it is then I can, *In every thing give thanks.* I don't thank God because I'm in trouble, but I do thank God that, even though I am in trouble, I have the resources to deal with the entire situation.

I remember again that a situation only becomes a problem if I do not have sufficient resources with which to meet it. If I do have the resources, then the situation becomes an incident!

There are thousands of Christians who have never learned to say "thank you" to God. Their prayers abound with desires and demands, for help and strength and blessing.

They miss the whole point of Philippians 4:4-7. Can you see, at a glance, what is wrong with this quotation?

> Rejoice in the Lord alway: and again I say, Rejoice.
> Let your moderation be known unto all men. The Lord is at hand.
> Be careful for nothing; but in every thing by prayer and supplication let your requests be made known unto God.
> And the peace of God, which passeth all understanding, shall keep your hearts and minds through Christ Jesus.

Does this seem correct to you? Is this what you do—you come in everything by prayer and supplication? But do you complain that the peace of God does not keep your heart and mind?

If this is so, you have missed out of your quotation two vital words. You can find them in verse 6, "Be careful for nothing; but in every thing by prayer and supplication *with thanksgiving* let your requests be made known unto God."

The two vital words here are, *with thanksgiving*. I bring my prayers and my supplications, but I bring them all *with thanksgiving*. The vitamin of "thankfulness" must be present in all my petitions and prayers.

When I pray with thankfulness, I pray from the position of strength. I know the glory of God's salvation. I rejoice in the forgiveness of sins and a home in heaven. But more than these, I am ever conscious that the blessed Lord is with me, dwelling in my heart and life through His Holy Spirit.

His presence guarantees His power—I know this. I rejoice in this and it is this for which I am eternally thankful.

78

If my prayers are only a constant round of asking, a cold barren emptiness of asking with no awareness of this vitamin of thankfulness, then I pray from a position of weakness and uncertainty.

The fact that I continue to ask denotes that I do not possess. It also indicates a condition of uncertainty—there is a doubt as to whether I will ever receive that for which I have asked so often.

Truly, so much of our prayers should be a calm, joyous, blessed profession of thankfulness. They should contain a confession in which we acknowledge the presence of our blessed Lord and in which we thank Him for His presence and His power.

Then, against the background of the sure presence of Christ, we line up our petitions and our requests. If we do this, we find a transformation taking place. We find that incidents and problems and pressures that seem so overwhelmingly large to us somehow slip into their proper proportion. Viewed against the sure presence of Christ and the eternal promises of God, our prayers take on a freshness of confidence inspired by all that is ours in Christ.

This is why in verse 7 we read, "And the peace of God, which passeth all understanding, shall keep your hearts and minds through Christ Jesus." We cannot experience the blessing of verse 7 until we fulfill the conditions of verse 6—*with thanksgiving.*

Notice what it is that keeps our hearts and minds—it is *the peace of God.* Therefore even though we may be in circumstances fraught with pressures and problems and difficulties, the peace of God can be our true tangible possession as we thank Him for all that is available and claim what is ours in the Lord Jesus.

ABILITY

"Victory" through the "Indwelling Christ" brought about by our "Thankfulness" in prayer should find an immediate demonstration of the vitamin of "Ability" in our daily living. But does it?

I have listened, over the years, to hundreds of testimonies from the lips of teenagers. I have seen young people rise to their feet with an earnest determination and then tell of what Christ has done for them. So often they have ended their testimony with a verse of Scripture in which they have affirmed their desire to go on and live for Christ.

The two Scriptures most frequently used are Galatians 2:20, "I am crucified with Christ," and Philippians 4:13, "I can do all things through Christ." Notice that these Scriptures say, *I am . . . I can.*

But, how abused these Scriptures become. The regular repetition of *I am* and *I can* produces a travesty of truth when one looks at the lives these same young people live. This is true of all of us.

The one thing missing is the vitamin of "Ability"—the ability to live up to this level and to experience this truth in daily living.

The vitamin of ability becomes real in our individual experience when we know and understand the "secret of the two laws." Campus Crusade has been used to bring the blessings of salvation to many hearts through the simple teaching of "The Four Spiritual Laws." Now, here are two more Spiritual Laws that can turn belief into behavior, and apathy into ability.

Romans 7:14-24 contains some of the saddest words in the Bible,

> For that which I do I allow not: for what I would, that do I not; but what I hate, that do I. . . . For I know that in me (that is, in my flesh), dwelleth no good thing: for to will is present with me; but how to perform that which is good I find not. For the good that I would I do not: but the evil which I would not, that I do . . . O wretched man that I am! who shall deliver me from the body of this death?

Is this the language of your life? Do you experience the wretched frustration of knowing how you ought to act, but of being continually unable to put it into practice? Do you find yourself doing that which you have earnestly repudiated, fought against, and condemned? This, in one way or another, is the daily experience of many Christians.

It is a help to view this behavior against the truth of verse 23. Here we read that there is "another law in my members, warring against the law of my mind, and bringing me into captivity to the law of sin which is in my members."

Notice the teaching that declares there is a *law of sin which is in my members*. Romans 8:2 calls it also, *the law of sin and death*. This is a "natural" law in every sense of the word.

It is "natural" for people to tell lies, to behave deceitfully, to have impure minds and to go into sin. When I was a principal of a school I never had to teach children to lie, to steal or to tell dirty stories. All these things came naturally.

In a similar way I Corinthians 2:14 says, "But the natural man receiveth not the things of the Spirit of God: for they are foolishness unto him: neither can he know them, because they are spiritually discerned." He cannot know them because he is spiritually dead.

This is where the law of sin and death operates. Just as there is a physical law of gravity, so there is a spiritual law of sin and death. The law of gravity is known to all of us, by continual daily experience. It is that force which pulls an object down to earth when it is released in space.

If I hold a book in my hand, then release my hold, the book falls to the floor. We are not surprised when this happens. We expect it to do so. We would be more amazed if it stayed there suspended in the air. This is the continual downward pull of gravity. This is why we and all other solid bodies stay on the ground.

What this downward pull of gravity does in the physical world, the law of sin and death effects in the moral and spiritual world. This is why lovely children become teenagers whose lives become filled with sin, lust and failure. There is a constant downward drag in every human heart and the civilization in which we now live offers increasing opportunities for this law to manifest itself.

So many young people are surrounded by a society which is geared to fasten on to the weaknesses of human nature, and then to drag them downward in a blinding mist of pleasure.

If this law of sin and death were the only force operating in the world today there would be no hope, no possibility of recovery, no chance of peace and joy and love. But the glory of the message of salvation is that there *is* a hope, and a blessed opportunity to defeat this downward pull.

Romans 8:2 tells of the other law which can overcome the sin and failure in the human heart, "For the law of the Spirit of life in Christ Jesus hath made me free from the law of sin and death."

The law of the *Spirit of life in Christ Jesus* is God's sure answer to the natural failure of the human heart.

Because the Lord Jesus indwells me through His Holy Spirit I am made *a partaker of the divine nature* (II Peter 1:4). My natural human nature can do nothing but fail—it is constantly subject to the law of sin and death. But now, because I have been born again and have received the Lord Jesus into my heart and life, I have the answer to sin and failure.

I can do nothing but fail; He can do nothing but succeed. He is always the victor over sin and death. Inasmuch as I commit my way, day by day, to Christ—in that much I can experience the upward pull of His victory.

This is where the vitamin of ability is known and experienced. See how the progression develops. First there is the "Victory" of Christ, then the "Indwelling Holy Spirit" to bring that victory into my heart and life. My "Thankfulness" is my daily acknowledgment of the One who never leaves me. Now the vitamin of "Ability" is the demonstration, in my own life, that these things are true, that *I am . . . I can.*

The Christian life is, in effect, the daily struggle between the downward pull of the law of sin and death and the upward thrust of the spirit of life in Christ Jesus. We can understand this more clearly if we consider the battle that is fought on every runway every time a plane takes off.

I experience this frequently when I fly to various places around the world. As the jet stands on the runway it will weigh altogether over 150 tons. The force of gravity will be holding it firmly on the ground. There will be no thought that it might float or blow over!

But at a given time the pilot will switch on the four jet engines—monsters of tremendous power. When he is ready he will taxi to the end of the long runway and the battle will begin. The force of gravity will fight hard to hold the huge plane on the ground. But the power put forth from the four jets will bring into operation the new law of aerodynamics. This new law is the truth that under certain conditions a heavy object can rise against the pull of gravity. This is the one and only way to defeat gravity.

As the plane rushes down the runway the battle is on—gravity versus aerodynamics—the downward pull versus the upward thrust. Suddenly the pilot has his moment of victory. He "pulls back his stick" and the plane leaps into the air. Gravity has been defeated by the power of aerodynamics.

I do not understand the mysterious law of aerodynamics—but I don't have to. All I have to do is to commit myself to the plane, to enter, sit down, relax and enjoy the wonders of modern flight.

In an amazing way the plane's victory becomes my victory. Because it overcame gravity, so can I—as long as I stay in the plane, committed to the plan and program of the plane.

I do not have to understand how the jet can fly this way. I do not have to help the plane in any way. Only two things are necessary from me—first, that I believe the plane is capable of making the flight, and second, that I commit myself to the plane. Remember, committing myself is not only believing that the plane can make it, but also climbing inside and yielding my whole·life to its plan and purpose.

In a way, this is the story of "the two laws" in the experience of every true Christian. There is a downward pull of the law of sin and death—always at work in our human nature, ever ready to drag us down and hold us down in sin and failure, fear and frustration.

But God has provided for us the blessed, wonderful law of the Spirit of life in Christ Jesus. I don't need to understand how such a glorious experience could be mine. All I need to do is to "climb into the plane," to commit my whole life to Christ. As I yield my whole being—thought, word and deed—to His power, plan and purpose, then His victory becomes my victory.

There needs to be a constant realization of this fact. I need to walk every step of the way committed to Christ. If I choose to go on my own way, to step out of the purpose and plan of Christ, then I also step out of His power. Instead of the upward thrust controlling my life, the downward pull takes over, and I become liable to all the failure and frustration that is "natural" to my human nature.

If this truth is to be worked out in my life, then I need to come to the place where I "climb into the plane." I need to make an act of committal in which I not only express my belief in the ability of Christ to give me success and victory, but I also actually make

84

His ability my ability, His power my power, His victory my victory.

Having begun with an act of committal, I need from then on to "stay in the plane"—to practice the activity of committal. In every situation and decision I need to affirm my dependence and to prove my affirmation by walking in humble obedience before Him. I need to remember that obedience is the proof of dependence.

When I fly I will be utterly obedient to that plane. If the plane wants to climb to six miles high—so will I. If it wants to travel at 600 mph—so will I. If the plane wants to descend and land—so will I. My committal to the plane will be complete.

These four wonderful spiritual vitamins are the basis for "The Plan for Maturity—For Me." I can be as mature as I want, as long as I nourish my soul on the vitamins of God.

A Prayer for Meditation

My Father, I am hungry for spiritual nourishment. I need vigor and vitality in my life and witness.

May I read, mark, learn and inwardly digest all that Thou hast for me.

Teach me to commit myself to the Lord Jesus Christ, then teach me to stay committed.

Encourage me to be obedient in all things.

As I go down the runway of life, may the victory of Christ become my victory—lifting me up against the downward pull of the world, the flesh and the devil.

May my life, as a result, be lived to His glory as the "life of Christ is made manifest in my mortal flesh," through Jesus Christ. Amen.

CHAPTER 7

JOSHUA—INCOMPLETE OBEDIENCE

IN CHAPTER 5 we considered God's dealings with Joshua. We saw the one condition of all blessing—that Joshua had, first, to recognize the presence of God in each situation, then, to practice the presence of God as the events crowded in.

In our last chapter we learned that obedience is the proof of dependence, and dependence is the secret of victory.

We can now move on to see the development of these two chapters spelled out in the experience of Joshua.

God had given Joshua a "promise," a "program" and a "power." This was to be the background against which his new life of leadership was to be lived. Joshua would have all the power he needed, as he looked to God for guidance and wisdom.

If we turn to Joshua 11:16-23 we see the results of that dependence. It is the list of battle honors won through the presence and power of God. Verse 16 begins, "So Joshua took all that land." Verse 17 ends with, "all their kings he took, and smote them, and slew them." Verse 18 reports that, "Joshua made war a long time with all those kings."

In verses 21 and 22 we read about the Anakims, who were the "giants" of the land. These are the people who were described by the ten spies on their return from the mission to spy out the land of Canaan. In

Numbers 13:33 they had said, "There we saw the giants, the sons of Anak, which come of the giants: and we were in our own sight as grasshoppers, and so we were in their sight."

In Joshua 11:21 we read, "And at that time came Joshua, and cut off the Anakims from the mountains ... Joshua destroyed them utterly with their cities."

Verse 22 continues, "There was none of the Anakims left in the land of the children of Israel: only in Gaza, in Gath, and in Ashdod, there remained."

"So Joshua took the whole land. ... And the land rested from war."

At first sight, verses 16-23 seem to present a glowing account of the victories won. This is especially so when we read the last six words, *and the land rested from war.* We get the impression that everything was a great success, the whole mission was successfully accomplished ... and they all lived happily ever after! But they did not, and if we examine verse 22 we will find out why they did not.

The land rested from war, but the peace they enjoyed was the peace before the storm. Verse 22 can teach us much on the subject of incomplete obedience when we remember the commands given to Joshua, the power at his disposal, and then we read this, "There was none of the Anakims left in the land of the children of Israel: only in Gaza, in Gath, and in Ashdod, there remained."

The verse begins with the words, *There was none of the Anakims left*—but this was not so. There were some of these deadly enemies left. It says so in the same verse, *only in Gaza, in Gath, and in Ashdod, there remained.*

This is the one blot on the perfect page of performance. Joshua did not deal with those three cities— Gaza, Gath and Ashdod. For some reason, unknown and unstated, he chose to allow these cities to stand, even though they were occupied by deadly enemies.

Were they too hard to conquer? No, because God had promised Joshua ... every place ... every day, victory could be his as he recognized the presence and power of God. We can find no apparent reason for this failure to wipe out the enemy. The only answer we can suggest is that this is a perfect example of the way we, today, yield our lives to Christ.

There are many of us who promise to yield our lives to Christ. We are moved with deep sincerity. We commit all that we are to Christ. We deal with all the enemies in our lives, and gladly we drive them out so that our lives will be completely for our Saviour and Lord. We take action against the habits, friendships, associations and other areas that would hold us back from full surrender.

Of us it could be said, *There was none of the Anakims left*—then we add, with a tiny whisper ... *only in Gaza, in Gath, and in Ashdod, there remained.* Like Joshua, we choose to allow unconquered areas to remain in our lives.

The great tragedy was that these three areas became the seeds of future sorrow and disaster. In Joshua's day they may have been small and insignificant, because, even though they were unconquered, the land rested from war. But the days came when the names Gaza, Gath and Ashdod brought fear and suffering to the children of Israel. The small neglected seeds grew to be monsters of overwhelming power.

As we continue our story and see what happened to unconquered Gaza, Gath and Ashdod, the tragedy will be brought home to us. None of these events and calamities need ever have happened. If only Joshua had taken time to deal effectively with all the Anakims, the people would have been spared the many days of shame and defeat.

And, of course, this is the lesson for us today. Our incomplete obedience to God, our holding back of special areas in our lives, brings a repetition of the story we are considering. The pet sins we retain can become the monsters that will bind us with chains.

The first city Joshua left unconquered was Gaza. If Joshua had done his job properly we would never have heard of the place again. The name Gaza means "The strong place."

We meet this city again in the Book of Judges. Chapters 14-16 of this book tell us the story of the man called Samson. The name Samson means the "Strong Man." Samson was a judge and judged Israel for twenty years. By his physical strength, and through the special guiding of God, he was able to preserve Israel from their enemies, the Philistines.

Judges 13:5 tells us what the angel of the Lord said to Samson's mother before he was conceived, "For, lo, thou shalt conceive, and bear a son; and no razor shall come on his head: for the child shall be a Nazarite unto God from the womb: and he shall begin to deliver Israel out of the hand of the Philistines." A Nazarite was a person especially set apart for God—in thought and word and deed.

Numbers 6:1-21 gives instructions for the life of a Nazarite. Three things were essential. First, the Nazarite could eat nothing that came from the vine—either grapes or juice (verse 3). Then the hair of his head was to be neither cut nor shaven (verse 5). Last, he could never come near a dead body, under any circumstances (verse 6). Notice how the angel emphasized to his mother that no razor was to be used on his head!

Samson's life recorded in Judges 14-16 is the pathetic story of a strong man who was able to overcome every enemy—except his own lusts. One by one the special marks of the Nazarite were pushed aside by Samson's natural desires. In Judges 14:5-9 he deliberately approached the carcass of a lion. Verse 10 of the same chapter describes the beginning of a seven day feast that Samson made for his own wedding, *for so used the young men to do*, a feast full of drinking and merriment.

Often he broke these same two distinguishing marks of a Nazarite, but he always remained true to the special command of the angel, *no razor shall come to his head*. He was God's strong man, God's chosen man, God's holy man, but the tragedy of his life was that Gaza, the strong place, was to prove too strong for him in the end.

Chapter 16 begins, "Then went Samson to Gaza, and saw there an harlot, and went in unto her. And it was told the Gazites, saying, Samson is come hither."

His lust finally took him to the "Strong Place." Here his enemies planned to kill him in the morning, but Samson escaped at midnight. However, this was the beginning of the end. The lords of the Philistines took action to accomplish his destruction.

Samson became involved with Delilah, and through her the lords of the Philistines sought his downfall. Each lord promised Delilah eleven hundred pieces of silver for the capture of Samson (Judges 16:5). Their bribes, acting on her deceit, finally led Samson to give away the secret of his strength—his uncut hair. This was the one remaining sign of a Nazarite, the visible sign of his complete allegiance and dedication to God.

So the "Strong Place" plotted against the "Strong Man" and won. Samson's hair was shaved off. When he was attacked by the enemy, "he awoke out of his sleep, and said, I will go out as at other times before, and shake myself. And he wist not that the LORD was departed from him" (verse 20).

He knew not that the Lord was departed from him! Oh, the empty loneliness, the awful tragedy of Samson! He had finally turned his back on God by repudiating his allegiance to God—and God had turned away from him.

Verse 21 describes the utter humiliation of Samson, "But the Philistines took him, and put out his eyes, and

90

brought him down to Gaza, and bound him with fetters of brass; and he did grind in the prison house." Thus Samson lost his strength, his sight, his liberty and his standing as a Nazarite of God.

When Samson was captured and humbled, Israel lost their leader. They as a people were overcome and overthrown and, worst of all, the name of the LORD was dragged in the dust. The Philistines sacrificed unto Dagon their god, they rejoiced and said, "Our god hath delivered Samson our enemy into our hand" (verse 23). In their eyes, Dagon had defeated Jehovah and the LORD was despised.

This, then, is part of the story of Gaza. It is a story of humiliation and degradation which has so many side effects—and all because of one man's unfaithfulness to God.

But, of course, the most important part of this story is that it need never have happened. If Joshua had done what God told him to do, Gaza would have disappeared from the pages of history for ever.

Remember, I Corinthians 10:6, 11 tells us that these stories are written for our warning, that we should take note and see whether any of us are behaving in the same way. How necessary is this warning of incomplete obedience from the lives of both Joshua and Samson!

Gath was another Anakim community that Joshua did not destroy. As you will remember, Gath along with Gaza and Ashdod, should have been wiped out. This was the second seed that was left to grow into a monster of oppression, and in this case it was a physical monster.

I Samuel 17 begins with Israel utterly frustrated and fearful of the Philistine champion—Goliath. Verse 4 gives this significant information, "And there went out a champion out of the camp of the Philistines, named Goliath, of Gath, whose height was six cubits and a span." Observe that this man came from Gath—the city that should have disappeared.

91

Because Joshua allowed Gath to stand, Goliath, several generations later, stood in open defiance and challenged the whole of Israel. In Joshua's day one man—strong in the strength of God—could have dealt with the entire city. Now in Goliath's day one man of Gath was able to deal with the entire nation. What a reversal of power!

Verses 8-10 give us the vaunting words of Goliath. He was so sure of himself. He could cry with fullest confidence, "I defy the armies of Israel this day; give me a man, that we may fight together." He knew he was invincible, and so did Saul and the men of Israel. "When Saul and all Israel heard those words of the Philistine, they were dismayed, and greatly afraid" (verse 11).

Verse 16 tells us, "And the Philistine drew near morning and evening, and presented himself forty days." The Israelites were brainwashed into defeat. They were at their wit's end to know how to deal with such a situation. King Saul should have been their champion. He was the tallest man they had (I Samuel 10:23), so that by size and sovereignty Saul should have faced the taunting Goliath. But Saul was dispirited and discouraged. Through his own disobedience to God he had willfully turned his back on Him. As a result, like Samson, he was left to stand in his own weakness.

Thus it was that when Israel's hopes were at their lowest God answered the challenge of Goliath. The giant had cried, *give me a man, that we may fight together*. God answered him, not by sending a full-grown man, but by sending a teenager.

Beginning at verse 20 we read of the coming of David. The important thing to realize is that he came fresh from the presence of God, "And David rose up early in the morning, and left the sheep with a keeper." We read in Luke 2:8, "And there were in the same country shepherds abiding in the fields, keeping watch over their flocks by night." These men saw the glory of the Lord in the Babe of Bethlehem on that first Christmas night. It is good to remember that David, hundreds of years before, had been abiding in those same fields, keeping watch over his flock by night. He was called from the presence of God to reveal the glory of the Lord to a broken, dispirited people.

David lived close to God. He had been anointed secretly by Samuel, and was aware of his divine calling. His heart and lips were filled with praises toward God, with words that found expression in the glorious Psalms of David. God was relevant to David, and day by day as he watched his sheep, he would commune with and draw closer to the Lord who was his Shepherd.

It was this young man, with his knowledge of the nearness of God, who was sent to deal with the man from Gath.

David arrived just in time to see the eightieth appearance of Goliath. He heard the proud boasting and saw the result, "And all the men of Israel, when they saw the man, fled from him, and were sore afraid" (verse 24).

As David spoke to the shattered Israelites he heard the full details of the failure of Saul's army. He heard also of the rewards that Saul was offering to anyone who would stand up to Goliath. Verse 25 gives details of the threefold reward—"riches, relationship and redemption."

David, coming from the presence of God, saw things differently than the frightened soldiers. They could only point to the towering monster and complain, "Look at him! Look how big he is! Look how much bigger he is than we are!" But David could say, "Yes, but look how much smaller he is than God!"

They were both viewing the same problem, but David, with his firm faith in God, was standing as Joshua had stood—with the "promise," the "program" and the "power."

David's confident words were reported to Saul, who

sent for him immediately (verse 31). Saul again underlined the human impossibility of David fighting Goliath. But David spoke of God's help on previous occasions—against a lion and a bear—and his faith was sure. "This uncircumcised Philistine shall be as one of them, seeing he hath defied the armies of the living God. . . . The LORD that delivered me out of the paw . . . he will deliver me out of the hand of this Philistine" (verse 37).

Saul was so impressed with David's assurance that he sent him to the battle. He tried to gird David in his armor but his offer was refused. David said, "I cannot go with these; for I have not proved them" (verse 39).

David went against Goliath armed with that which had given him victory before—a sure sense of the "promise," the "program" and the "power." His material weapons were the simplicity of five smooth stones. They were in his hand, but he was safe in the hands of God.

When Goliath, the man of Gath, saw David, the man of God, he despised and disdained him. Goliath saw only "a youth, and ruddy, and of a fair countenance." But David said, "I come . . . in the name of the LORD of hosts, the God of the armies of Israel, whom thou hast defied" (verse 45). David had the invisible weapon of "the name of the LORD of hosts."

David's words in verses 46 and 47 represent the highest quality of faith. He who had the promise and the power told his enemy what would soon follow.

The Philistine drew near, but David hastened and ran to meet him. What quiet confidence! With the utmost assurance David stated, "the battle is the LORD's, and he will give you into our hands" (verse 47). Notice the words *our hands,* not "my hands." David was not claiming anything for himself. He was God's man, representing Israel.

One of the most beautiful aspects of this story is the

demonstration of the quiet intimacy between God and David. God was completely relevant to David.

The rest of the story is so well-known—the defeat of Goliath—the sudden renewed enthusiasm of the army of Israel and the glorious deliverance that came that day. It was all because of David, God's man.

We have been considering this story as an example of the result of incomplete obedience. We have seen the boasting pride of Goliath as the result of Joshua's failure to deal with Gath.

This failure is seen in greater depth if we turn to II Samuel 21:18-22. This chapter records the further battles of David when, as the king, he sought to subdue all his enemies. It tells how Goliath had four brothers, all of whom were of great stature. One in particular had "on every hand six fingers, and on every foot six toes, four and twenty in number" (v. 20).

Referring to Goliath's other brothers verse 22 says, "These four were born to the giant in Gath, and fell by the hand of David, and by the hand of his servants." This shows us two things. First, that there was a breed of giants living in Gath. Second, that when David faced Goliath on that fateful day there were four more brothers in the Philistine ranks.

This is surely David's reason for taking the five smooth stones. He only needed one, but, if the other brothers had attempted to avenge the death of Goliath, David was equipped to deal with them. When God sent David to the battle, He gave him sufficient resources to deal with any eventuality.

This can also be true of us, as shown in I Corinthians 15:57, *But thanks be to God, which giveth us the victory through our Lord Jesus Christ.* All of our resources are in Christ, but our failure to appropriate all that "He is" puts us in the same position as Saul and his army. We are God's people, but are unable to cope with the situation.

The third Anakim center that Joshua left standing

was Ashdod. As we re-examine these three places we find that Gaza was the place of defeat, Gath the place of defiance, and Ashdod the place of defilement.

I Samuel 4 recounts the miserable attempt of the Israelites to overcome the Philistines at Ebenezer. The first attack was a failure in which Israel lost about four thousand men (verse 2).

At that time Eli was the priest at Shiloh, and his sons, Hophni and Phinehas, were the officiating priests.

These sons were utter failures in every sense of the word. I Samuel 2:12 says, "Now the sons of Eli were sons of Belial; they knew not the LORD." What an amazing condemnation! They wore the priestly garments, and performed the priestly functions, but they did not know the LORD. Their behavior, as recorded in verses 13-17 and 22-25, made mockery of anything holy.

The tragic result of the ministry of these ungodly sons is seen in the behavior of the elders of Israel in I Samuel 4:3. After the first defeat by the Philistines these elders said, "Let us fetch the ark of the covenant of the LORD out of Shiloh unto us, that, when it cometh among us, it may save us out of the hand of our enemies." What a crazy idea this was, but how it demonstrated the absence of true worship and the absence of God's presence.

David, in our previous story, could speak of the Lord being with him. These men spoke about an "it"— *when it cometh . . . it may save us*. They became "it-ites" and perished.

Verse 4 tells how Hophni and Phinehas joined the "it-ites," and verse 5 records the excitement in the Israelite camp when the Ark appeared in their midst: "all Israel shouted with a great shout, so that the earth rang again." The presence of "it" brought them courage.

But notice the reaction of the Philistines as recorded in verse 7. When they heard the noise, "the Philistines were afraid, for they said, God is come into the camp." What an amazing situation! The pagan Philistines recognized the Ark as the presence of God, while the Israelites were getting excited over "it."

The result of the next attack was an utter and complete disaster. Israel was crushed, "for there fell of Israel thirty thousand footmen" (verse 10). Hophni and Phinehas perished as did Eli. But the supreme tragedy was the capture, by the Philistines, of the holy Ark of God.

Chapter 5 begins with these awful words, "And the Philistines took the ark of God, and brought it from Ebenezer unto Ashdod." That place which Joshua overlooked in his initial conquest grew so powerful that it could capture the Holiest of all—the Ark of God, the mercy seat of Jehovah—and this is the irony of it all.

Ebenezer means "Hitherto hath the Lord helped us," but these wicked men had turned their backs on God. All they wanted was a religion that would make them respectable and successful. All they found was bitter sorrow!

The name Ashdod means "fortress," and to this seat of the enemy the Ark was taken. The Ark was placed in the temple of Dagon, a vile, filthy heathen idol. Later, Dagon fell because of the judgment of God, but not before the LORD was subjected to defilement and disgrace.

The theme continues to remain the same—this need never have happened if only, at the beginning, Joshua had dealt with all the Anakims.

We meet the name Ashdod in strange circumstances later on in the Book of Nehemiah. The earlier chapters of this book record the faithful work of Nehemiah as he strove to rebuild the walls of Jerusalem. We read of the enemies he met—Sanballat and Tobiah the Ammonite. As his work prospered, we read these words in Nehemiah 4:7, 8, "But it came to pass, that when Sanballat, and Tobiah . . . and the Ashdodites, heard that the walls of Jerusalem were made up . . . then they were very wroth. And conspired all of them together to come and to fight against Jerusalem."

Here we find the neglected Ashdod preparing openly to fight against Jerusalem from the outside. But worse was to come.

Nehemiah had to leave his work at Jerusalem for some time, but when he returned he was horrified to see the infiltration of the enemy within the city of Jerusalem.

Nehemiah 13:4 records that, "Eliashib the priest, having the oversight of the chamber of the house of our God, was allied unto Tobiah: And he had prepared for him a great chamber."

Verses 23, 24 tell us that, "In those days also saw I Jews that had married wives of Ashdod . . . . And their children spake half in the speech of Ashdod, and could not speak in the Jews' language."

Imagine this fantastic infiltration of Ashdod right into the holy city of Jerusalem. Some Jewish men had married pagan women, but the pagan women had brought their cultures and their language with them. Therefore, within the walls of Jerusalem, a generation of young people was growing up who could not speak the Jews' language. All they knew was the speech of Ashdod, the place of defilement, with all its unholy, ungodly associations.

This is a true picture of what is happening today in many churches and homes in our land. The impurity of Ashdod finds its way everywhere, even into the speech of the people.

This study is not a blast against joy and happiness and the many things that can make our faith attractive and wholesome. But, as I Corinthians 10 reminds us, it is a challenge to all of us to see how far the "promise," the "program" and the "power" have been put into effect in our own immediate context. Failure to deal with a known area of sin will surely lead to a harvest of hopeless struggling.

Gaza produced a generation of wealthy lords of the Philistines. Gath produced a generation of giants. Ashdod brought secret defilement reaching like a cancer into all areas of holy living. But none of it need ever have arisen, if only Joshua had done what God told him to do.

In like manner, many of the trials and difficulties and problems we face today are of our own begetting. It is easy to blame the world and the pressures of our modern society for the failure within the church and within our own lives. Not only is it easy, it is also a comfortable excuse by which I can absolve myself and rationalize my fruitlessness and failure.

But, when all is said and done, it is still true in many cases that, as it was with Joshua, so it is with us. If we would only get on our knees and claim the promise, carry out the program, and experience the power in every area of our personality—emotions, mind or intellect, and will—then we would be spared the hurt and bitter sorrow of incomplete obedience.

A Prayer for Meditation

O Heavenly Father, I stand appalled at the record of history. I see the uselessness of trying without trusting, and the stupidity of complaining without committing.

Teach me to recognize more and more the holiness of God. Then teach me to relate my daily living to that same holiness.

May the words of David be my prayer: Search me, O God, and know my heart: try me, and know my thoughts: And see if there be any wicked way in me, and lead me in the way everlasting. For Jesus' sake. Amen.

CHAPTER 8

THE PLAN FOR MATURITY—
THROUGH ME

left off
march 13

IN CHAPTER 6, as we considered "The Plan for Me," we opened up the idea of spiritual vitamins. We realized the need for those special items in our spiritual diet that would put a crispness into our living, and a boldness into our witnessing.

We considered "**V**ictory" as the basis on which our life is to be lived; the "**I**ndwelling Holy Spirit" as the One who would make that victory possible. "**T**hanksgiving," we found, was the means whereby the indwelling Christ was recognized and released in our daily living. "**A**bility" in our lives was seen when the downward pull of spiritual gravity was counteracted by the upward thrust of "the law of the Spirit of life in Christ Jesus."

All these truths were specifically *for* me. I was the one in whom the victory was made manifest. We can now go on to consider the remaining three letters in the word, M-I-N, and see how they, in turn, are essentially to operate *through* me.

The failures we considered in the last chapter can only be prevented by the continual application of the positive aspect of these "vitamins"—through me.

MERCY

This is a simple word we know so well—but use so little. There are quite a number of such simple, Scriptural words which somehow get left out of daily conversation. There is little evidence of mercy in the busy world in which we live. Few people want mercy these days. We are much more concerned in getting our rights, in being equal, and in demonstrating our personal attitudes and aspirations.

Mercy is really love in operation. Because God is love, then mercy is the way in which that love is made manifest to us.

This world knows little of "love"—that basic quality of real Christian love—and as a result it is not interested in mercy. This vitamin of mercy is an essential in the plan for Christian maturity, especially for a maturity that is going to be evidenced through me.

The fact that my approach to life is one full of mercy, will, of itself, make an unusual impact on all around me. It is sometimes said of evangelical Christians that there is a lack of tender compassion in their outlook to the world around them. They are so busy witnessing and winning souls for Christ that they have little time for showing simple acts of loving-kindness— just for the sake of being gracious. Kindness might even be mistaken for compromise.

Mercy, too, seems to be considered unnecessary between some Christians—inasmuch as it is seldom demonstrated. It is taken for granted that we all love each other—with a very small "l." But, somehow we feel we should not have to show mercy to our brothers and sisters in Christ. No one says as much in so many words, but "actions speak louder than words."

I have counseled with several Christians who have been deeply hurt and wounded, simply because someone did not show mercy. Mercy certainly is the prerogative of God, but it should also be the plan for every true believer.

Let us think first of *The Reality of Mercy* and see how important this is in the Word of God.

II Corinthians 1:3 says, "Blessed be God, even the

Father of our Lord Jesus Christ, the Father of mercies, and the God of all comfort." What a blessed concept that is! God is the *Father of mercies.*

Ephesians 2:4, speaking of our salvation, says, "But God, who is rich in mercy." The *Amplified Bible* brings out the exalting sense of the words, "But God! So rich is He in His mercy!"

Titus 3:5 emphasizes that, "Not by works of righteousness which we have done, but according to his mercy he saved us." Observe how, in each case, it is truly love in operation.

Peter was a man who experienced much of the mercy of God and of Christ. He could say in I Peter 1:3, "Blessed be the God and Father of our Lord Jesus Christ, which according to his abundant mercy hath begotten us again unto a lively hope by the resurrection of Jesus Christ from the dead." No wonder he speaks of the *abundant mercy.*

A lovely picture of the reality of mercy in the Old Testament is found in II Samuel 9. David is firmly and safely on the throne of Israel. All his enemies have been subdued and he is now in a position to exercise his power as king of Israel. Verse 1 tells of the quality of tender compassion in his heart, "And David said, Is there yet any that is left of the house of Saul, that I may shew him kindness for Jonathan's sake?"

There was one, a son of Jonathan named Mephibosheth, who dwelt in Lo-debar. Lo-debar means "no pasture"—a desolate place. Mephibosheth had been lame since the age of five, but David sought him out, raised him up and restored to him the possessions of Saul. He also made him to eat at his table "as one of the King's sons" (verse 11).

This is mercy of the highest order. It exalts the giver and brings nothing but blessing to the recipient. This is a true picture of God's mercy to us who were also in a desolate place and powerless to help ourselves.

The *Reality of Mercy* is the expression of God's love

102

toward us. The *Result of Mercy* is our response to God. In Romans 15 the Holy Spirit is moving Paul to encourage Christian behavior. He writes in verse 1, "We then that are strong ought to bear the infirmities of the weak, and not to please ourselves." He goes on in verse 5 to speak of "the God of patience and consolation."

Verse 9 has a special challenge to all of us. Having written of the grace and kindness of God Paul continues, "And that the Gentiles might glorify God for his mercy." This is where we become involved in the story. The *Result of Mercy* is our response to God and this should be a determined attitude on our part to *glorify God for His mercy*.

How is this to be carried out? This is seen in our third thought concerning mercy. First the *Reality of Mercy,* then the *Result of Mercy* which leads us to the *Response to Mercy.*

My response to God's mercy is described in Romans 12:1, 2, "I beseech you therefore, brethren, by the mercies of God, that ye present your bodies a living sacrifice, holy, acceptable unto God, which is your reasonable service. And be not conformed to this world: but be ye transformed by the renewing of your mind, that ye may prove what is that good, and acceptable, and perfect, will of God."

This precious vitamin of mercy is going to be seen in a twofold way: in my response to God, and in my reaction to those around me, whoever they may be.

My response to God will be seen in this revolutionary act of *presenting my body a living sacrifice, holy, acceptable unto God*. This is something often talked about, discussed and dissected, but is not often done. If I am conscious of the mercy of God, and if this mercy really touches the depths of my being, then I will have only one response—to present my body a living sacrifice.

The lack of response to presenting our bodies to the

103

Lord is surely our lack of appreciation of the mercy of God. The reality of that mercy and the result of that mercy sends us in worship and humble adoration to present all that we are—with no reservations.

We can pick out a central theme in these two verses as follows, *present . . . that ye may prove.* This is something many young people need to appreciate. I have counseled with many concerning the "will of God" for their lives. They have a sincere interest in knowing God's will, but they have reversed the order of this theme. They want to know what God's will might be. Then, if it appeals to them, they will present their bodies. There is almost a sense of bargaining with God.

The only way to prove the will of God to be always good, always acceptable, and always perfect is to seek to appreciate more and more the mercies of God, and then in glad response, to yield my body a living sacrifice. The consequences, whatever they may be, can never add up to the infinite mercies of God so freely bestowed upon me.

Thus it is I need this precious vitamin of "Mercy"— to glorify God and to gladden the hearts of all whom I contact. Without it there will be a lack of sweet tenderness in my daily life. I may be absolutely correct in all my ways, but it will be a cold correctness, devoid of that warm glow that characterized the Lord Jesus when He was here on earth.

INHERITANCE

If tomorrow's mail brought you a letter from an attorney telling you that some unknown relative had left you an inheritance of $100,000, many things would surely happen. After you had recovered from the shock, your new resources would permit you to move into a new quality of living, because you would have a new capacity for living. Wouldn't that be marvelous?— or would it?

The strange thing about our next vitamin, "our daily Inheritance," is that these new things have come to pass in our lives. They do so daily. We *can* experience a new quality of living, because we *do* now have a new capacity for living, due to our new resources. Yet so many of us go on living the same spiritual preinheritance lives. We live in the same spiritual shack, wear the same spiritual rags and engage in the same drudgery of daily survival—and all the while we are spiritual millionaires.

Ephesians 1:11 reminds us of our spiritual heritage. Paul was speaking of the wonder and the glory of Christ, then he added, "In whom also we have obtained an inheritance." We have this amazing declaration, that Jesus Christ, in all His riches of power, wisdom and blessing, is our inheritance—day by day, and moment by moment. Verse 14 confirms this by stating that the Holy Spirit Himself is "the earnest of our inheritance." The word *earnest* here means "the first installment."

The Holy Spirit is the One who represents Christ in our daily experience (John 14:26). Christ indwells us in the Person of His Holy Spirit (Romans 8:9).

Paul lived up to the inheritance he possessed. We read in Philippians 1:21, "For to me to live is Christ" and in 4:13, "I can do all things through Christ which strengtheneth me." Paul drew heavily on his spiritual resources, but he was never overdrawn. What the Lord Jesus Christ was in the experience of Paul He can be also in our experience, as by faith we continue to realize the infinite riches we have through the indwelling Christ.

In Ephesians 1:7 Paul speaks of the Lord Jesus, "In whom we have redemption through his blood, the forgiveness of sins, according to the riches of his grace." This is the wonder of our redemption. It is all through Christ, and it is all truly and sincerely appreciated by every born-again believer. This is what Christ did *for* me when He died on the cross, and for this I praise His holy Name and bow in worship and thankful adoration.

The blessed wonder of our "Inheritance" is all that the Lord Jesus can be *in* me—not only *for* me on the cross, but *in* me through His Holy Spirit. The appropriation and application of this "spiritual vitamin" is sure to lead to a robust and purposeful Christian life. A realization of my untold resources in Christ brings the rest of life into a truer perspective. My sense of values becomes much more honest and sincere as I evaluate my daily life against the glory of my inheritance in Christ.

But, not only does the vitamin of inheritance put me into the good of a new relationship with Christ, it also challenges me into a growing awareness of the relationship the Lord Jesus has with me. Ephesians 1:15 gives us the beginning of a precious prayer of Paul. In this prayer Paul is asking *the God and Father of our Lord Jesus Christ* to do something special for these Ephesian Christians. What he asked for them is what is so much needed in our hearts and lives.

In verse 18 he asked, "The eyes of your understanding being enlightened; that ye may know what is the hope of his calling, and what the riches of the glory of his inheritance in the saints."

Notice this second use of the word "inheritance," but see how different it is from that in verse 11. In verse 11 it was "my inheritance in Christ"; in verse 18 it is "his inheritance in me." The vitamin of inheritance has a two-way effect. First, it exposes all the resources of Christ to me. Second, it presents all that I am to Him.

The full benefit of this vitamin is only seen when I live in the good of this double thrust. The fact is that many of us are prepared, after we are made aware of the truth, to recognize the intimate blessing of the indwelling Christ, and, as a result, we draw upon our inheritance in Him. However, few of us are prepared to go the entire length of this teaching and respond to the

106

simple fact that the Lord Jesus also has an inheritance—in us. To do so could be a costly business—it could hurt, it may harm our pet plans and ambitions.

We saw, as we began this chapter, that these next three "vitamins" would lead us to "The Plan for Maturity—Through Me." It is not just what God would do *for* me, but what He could do *through* me.

The vitamin of "Mercy," we saw, would be seen in a twofold way—in my response to God and in my reaction to those around me, whoever they may be. In a similar way, the powerful vitamin of "Inheritance" will only be evident in all its fullness in my life when I am drawing on all the potential of Christ, and when my humanity is placed unreservedly at His disposal.

The Story of the Lost Inheritance

The Old Testament is God's Picture Book in which He shows and teaches many of the lessons we need to learn in our daily Christian experience.

One such lesson is the story of the lost inheritance. In Genesis 15 God is dealing specifically with Abram whom He had called out of Ur of the Chaldees. In verse 1 God said, "Fear not, Abram: I am thy shield, and thy exceeding great reward." In verse 7 God disclosed His purpose to Abram, "And he said unto him, I am the LORD that brought thee out of Ur of the Chaldees, to give thee this land to inherit it." Notice that God was here promising an inheritance to Abram.

In Genesis 28 Isaac blessed Jacob before he departed to visit Laban. In doing so, in verse 4, he said, "And give thee the blessing of Abraham, to thee, and to thy seed with thee; that thou mayest inherit the land wherein thou art a stranger, which God gave unto Abraham." Here the promise of the inheritance was passed on from Abraham to Jacob and to his descendants.

In Leviticus 20 God was speaking unto the people through His servant Moses. In verse 24 we read, "But I have said unto you, Ye shall inherit their land, and I will give it unto you to possess it, a land that floweth with milk and honey: I am the LORD your God, which have separated you from other people." Here again is the unconditional promise of God. First it was to a man, then it was to a family, now it is to a nation. The promise was an inheritance from God.

The story of the deliverance of the children of Israel from Egypt was all part of the story of the lost inheritance. Their inheritance was Canaan, a land flowing with milk and honey. But the tragedy of their deliverance was the way in which they fell short of God's plan.

They were delivered *from* Egypt, but they were never delivered *into* Canaan. Deuteronomy 6:20-25 tells what a Jewish father had to say to his son, "Then thou shalt say unto thy son, We were Pharaoh's bondmen in Egypt; and the LORD brought us out of Egypt with a mighty hand: . . . And he brought us out from thence, that he might bring us in, to give us the land which he sware unto our fathers."

The purpose of their redemption was to bring them out of their bondage into their inheritance. The resultant tragedy of their deliverance was that they had enough faith to get out of Egypt—but not enough to enter Canaan and claim their inheritance.

The Book of Deuteronomy was written *in the wilderness* (1:1) at the end of forty wasted years of wandering. Moses could say in 12:9, "For ye are not as yet come to the rest and to the inheritance, which the LORD your God giveth you." They had the deliverance—but not the inheritance. Because they had not the inheritance, they did not enjoy the rest of God.

I Corinthians 10 tells us to examine this story carefully and see if it depicts our own experience. Are we sure of our redemption from sin and of our deliverance from guilt? But more so, have we entered into our own special inheritance—the fullness of the boundless resources of Christ? Israel's inheritance was *a land flowing with milk and honey.* Our inheritance is *a Land flowing with might and happiness.*

The story of the lost inheritance is simply that Israel chose to wander in a wilderness of want, instead of entering into all that God had for them. How true this is in many Christian lives today! Many people are wandering in their private wilderness of want, instead of entering into the sufficiency of Christ.

But this story had an unhappy sequel in the history of the children of Israel. Because they did not enter into their inheritance, God was not able to enter into His inheritance. Deuteronomy 4:20 says, "But the LORD hath taken you, and brought you forth out of the iron furnace, even out of Egypt, to be unto him a people of inheritance, as ye are this day." In Deuteronomy 9:29, Moses, when speaking to God, said, "Yet they are thy people and thine inheritance." In Deuteronomy 32:9 Moses stated, "For the LORD's portion is his people; Jacob is the lot of his inheritance."

Just as Israel had an inheritance—so had God. The children of Israel were God's peculiar inheritance. *For* them He wrought all the miracles of Egypt as He effected their deliverance. *Through* them He was going to work out all His counsels and purposes. But when Israel refused to enter Canaan and claim their inheritance, God was denied the possibility of using them as His inheritance.

The story of the lost inheritance is the story of a double loss, and this is what Ephesians 1:11 and 18 is telling us. If I exclude the vitamin of inheritance from my daily spiritual diet I lose out—and so does God!

Inasmuch as I recognize all that the Lord Jesus can be *in* me through His indwelling Holy Spirit, and, also, inasmuch as I realize that I am the vehicle through whom He is going to fulfill His purposes—then, in that much do I appropriate my inheritance in Him, and in that much is Christ able to operate through my yielded life.

NEW CREATURE

Much of the successful sale of physical vitamins comes because of the approach used in advertising. People find it hard to resist the offer of a new capacity for daily living. The harried housewife is eager to gain that lasting quality of physical strength that will enable her to cope with family, friends and frustrations.

The overworked, overstrained businessman is interested in a product that promises to restore his peace of mind, and which also offers increased abilities to think fast, plan wisely and remain buoyant throughout the day.

In saying this, we thank God for all the skills of medical research which have enabled scientists to unlock new secrets and release to us those precious vitamins which do so much for so many people.

It is good to know that God has for us a spiritual vitamin which does all this and much more. II Corinthians 5:17 contains these wonderful words, "Therefore if any man be in Christ, he is a new creature: old things are passed away; behold, all things are become new." Other translations say, "he is a new creation."

This is the culminating glory of being a true Christian. I am "in Christ" and Christ is "in me" and, as a result, I am a new creation. Notice the tenses used in this verse. It is not a promise of things to come, but is a proclamation of that which is true, here and now: *he is . . . old things are . . . all things are.*

This is in keeping with the words of the Lord Jesus in John 5:24, "Verily, verily, I say unto you, He that heareth my word, and believeth on him that sent me, hath everlasting life, and shall not come into condemnation; but is passed from death unto life." *He hath everlasting life . . . he is passed.* This passing from spiritual death into everlasting life is the act and process of becoming a new creation.

I remember seeing an effective TV commercial which sought to illustrate the amazing effects of a certain vitamin on a tired mother. The mother was seen in an exhausted condition, collapsed in a chair. She then took the vitamin and, a few moments later, we saw the dramatic effects of its mysterious power. The tired body had been slumped in the chair, but out of this abject weariness there stepped the same woman full of life and abounding with energy. The success of the advertisement lay in showing the same woman, at the same time, in the two conditions—one still an exhausted wreck (what she had been)—the other a miracle of dynamic energy (what she had become).

This precious spiritual vitamin of experiencing and demonstrating "being a new creation" is the culminating wonder and joy of being a born-again believer. What the scientists offer as a physical experience is multiplied a thousand times in every area of the human personality. Unless a person has experienced the sheer joy of being a new creature in Christ, words would fail to convey the multiplicity of blessings that come, seen and unseen, moment by moment, and day by day.

All the previous spiritual vitamins, the "Victory," the realization of the "Indwelling Holy Spirit," the "Thanksgiving," the "Ability," the "Mercy" and the "Inheritance," all lead to, and from, this wondrous fact—that I am a new creation even while living in this same body and in these same circumstances.

It is satisfying to know that God is not interested in "patching up" people. Humanism and other similar philosophies are dedicated to "making the best of a bad situation," to patching up broken personalities and stopping the holes through which the sea is pouring in. This is not God's way of doing things.

The God of redemption is the God of creation, and His hand is seen at work in both areas. God never gathers the old leaves that have fallen from the trees, to wash them and press them so that they look fresh and clean. God never puts old leaves back on the trees. His springtime is the demonstration of "a new creation" in the world of nature, in every area of living things.

As the life flows again within the heart of the tree, so the evidences of the new life appear in the new buds and the new leaves. The tree becomes a demonstration of new life, and God is glorified in His creation.

In a much more wonderful manner, when I have been born again through believing in the shed blood of Christ on Calvary's cross, then I, too, receive a new quality of life. I John 5:11, 12 assures me that, "this is the record, that God hath given to us eternal life, and this life is in his Son. He that hath the Son hath life; and he that hath not the Son of God hath not life."

This is why, and how, I am a new creation in Christ. I am a new creation because I now possess a new quality of life—nothing less than the indwelling Christ.

The fact and the experience of the incoming Christ is so completely revolutionary that, as II Corinthians 5:17 says, *old things are passed away*. The "old things"—the old desires, the old ambitions, the old approach to life and living, the old capacity to act and react to situations and circumstances—all these, and a thousand others are passed away. This is not the proof of a new negative approach to life—full of don'ts and can'ts—but it is the laying aside of a tired weariness that was slumped in the chair of hopelessness.

The same verse goes on to add, "behold, all things are become new." Notice the word *behold* and remember how it was used by the angel to Joseph, "Behold, a virgin shall be with child" (Matthew 1:23); by the angel to Mary, "behold, thou shalt conceive in thy womb" (Luke 1:31); and by the angel to the shepherds, "behold, I bring you good tidings of great joy" (Luke 2:10). Could you *behold and see* that *the Lord hath done great things for thee?* Not only are you born again,

112

but in the very experiencing of this *all things are become new*.

Notice the simple comparison, the *old things* are passed away, however many or few they were, but *all things* are become new. As a new creation in Christ I have, here and now, not only the desires for new things but the capacity to experience them and carry them out.

Whether this becomes true in my actual experience depends upon my reaction to this precious vitamin of being a new creation. If I put it to work in my daily Christian life, by the faith of a simple committal to Christ every step of the way, then gradually and surely will this new life become apparent.

It does not come about by my putting on an act, trying to copy Jesus or live like Him—that would be just the works of the flesh. Romans 8:8 tells us, "So then they that are in the flesh cannot please God"—whether the "flesh" be "bad" or "good."

The resulting experience in my daily life would be such as Paul describes in II Corinthians 4:10, 11, "that the life also of Jesus might be made manifest in our body ... that the life also of Jesus might be made manifest in our mortal flesh." Notice the life of Jesus is *made manifest*. I do not manifest it, or try to make it manifest—the life is made manifest. The trees do not try to grow leaves. The rising sap, which is the new life of the tree, makes itself evident through the display of new leaves.

Remember also that there is no Spring for a dead tree. If I am still spiritually dead, never having been born again, then I can never demonstrate the evidences of a new creation. I am still a dead tree, however beautifully the sun may shine.

We have already established in our thinking the truth that we are new creatures, here and now, that we are passed from death unto life. In this respect it is interesting to turn to Revelation 21 and to read of the new heaven and the new earth. Verse 5 says, "And he that sat upon the throne said, Behold, I make all things new." Notice the phrase, *I make all things new.* It is the *things* that will be made new, not the people. Observe also II Peter 3:13, 14, "Nevertheless we, according to his promise, look for new heavens and a new earth, wherein dwelleth righteousness. Wherefore, beloved, seeing that ye look for such things."

God is making the people new, here and now, through the wonder of the new creation. God will make all things new in His own good time.

Here then is "The Plan for Maturity—Through Me." We have spoken of the "vitamins" that can make spiritual babies grow into men and women of God who, in their turn, can be warriors for God and living testimonies to the value of a faith that can cope with everything—every place—every day.

A PRAYER FOR MEDITATION

Dear Father, how refreshing it is to know that the Christian faith is not a boring experience, but a blessed example of all that Christ can be for me, and in me.

May these "vitamins" become an essential part of my diet.

As they move within my spiritual blood stream may the evidences of a new creation be seen in me.

May I manifest mercy in a world that has forgotten to care.

May I live in all the wealth of my inheritance in Christ.

May I respond equally, as I see myself as His inheritance.

May the "old things" continue to pass and fade away, and may the "all things new" be, all for Jesus, in whose name I pray. Amen.

CHAPTER 9

THE BOOK OF RAHAB—SAVED TO LIVE

THUS FAR WE HAVE BEEN considering the twofold work of the Lord Jesus Christ for the believer. We have considered the work of Christ *for* me, when He died on the cross in my place and paid the price of my sins. We read of this in I Peter 2:24, "Who his own self bare our sins in his own body on the tree, that we, being dead to sins, should live unto righteousness: by whose stripes ye were healed."

Then we have considered the work of Christ *in* me, through His indwelling Holy Spirit. This is spoken of in Colossians 1:26, 27, "the mystery which hath been hid from ages and from generations, but now is made manifest to his saints: to whom God would make known what is the riches of the glory of this mystery among the Gentiles; which is Christ in you, the hope of glory."

Observe that the death of Christ *for* me on the cross qualifies me to die, and go to heaven as a forgiven sinner, saved by the blood of His cross.

Observe also that the life of the risen Christ *in* me, indwelling me through His Holy Spirit, qualifies me, as a forgiven sinner, to live here and now, in this hostile, evil world system. The Lord Jesus said in John 14:19, "because I live, ye shall live also." Because He died, I die; because He lives, I live.

We have seen, also, that Christian maturity is a growing experience and demonstration of the life of Christ at work in the heart and life of the believer. This

115

is especially seen in Colossians 1:28 where Paul says, "Whom we preach, warning every man, and teaching every man in all wisdom; that we may present every man perfect in Christ Jesus." Notice that verse 28 begins with a "whom" not with a "what."

Paul did not preach a "what," or an "ethic," or a "program," or even "religion"—he preached a "whom." The "whom" of verse 28 is found in verse 27—that is *Christ in you*.

So the message Paul preached concerned not only Christ *for* me, but Christ *in* me. Notice the progression of preaching in verse 28—*warning every man—teaching every man—presenting every man perfect*. The word "perfect" is better translated "mature." This is the very word we have been considering in our own Christian experience.

We see that Paul had a threefold use of the word *every man*. He warned everyone, taught everyone and expected everyone to grow up into maturity. But notice that maturity is based on the "whom"—"Christ in you." This is so important, and yet so often overlooked by Christians.

It is possible to live my Christian life knowing only Christ for me, on the cross. When this is so I am a saved soul. I go to heaven when I die, but I am not equipped to face a world which is hostile to God and to His Christ.

It is only when I go on, to grow on to maturity—that maturity which is based on the work of Christ in me day by day—that I can be all that God would have me to be.

We have considered this in depth in our previous chapter when we thought of the spiritual vitamins that can charge our complete Christian concept.

We now turn to the Old Testament and find the same teaching set forth in story form. The story we will consider we have entitled "The Book of Rahab."

We have already looked into the "Book of Joshua"

in chapters 3, 5 and 7 of this book. Notice the hidden emphasis in the title of the book. It is the "Book of Joshua"—the story of what God did with his life. In one sense your present life is "The Book of You," and we have already seen, in chapter 4, that at the Judgment Seat of Christ this personal "Book of You" will be the subject of discussion and examination by Christ Himself.

With this idea of the "Book of You" in mind, let us go on to consider the story we have of Rahab—the story of her life—"The Book of Rahab." We will find this to be a tremendous illustration of the very things we have been considering thus far.

We first read of Rahab in the Bible in Joshua 2. As we read these twenty-four verses she emerges as a most remarkable person. Verse 1 speaks of the two spies who were sent to spy out Jericho, "they went, and came into an harlot's house, named Rahab, and lodged there." Bible scholars tell us that Rahab's home was the local inn at which all travelers could stay. This may be so, but the fact remains that she is known throughout the Bible as Rahab the harlot, or Rahab the prostitute.

Wherever we meet her she is stuck with this awful name. Rahab was the lowest of the low in the eyes of the Jews—a woman—a pagan—a prostitute. But it was this woman in whose life God choose to do marvelous things as He revealed Himself to her, and then through her.

Verse 3 of this chapter tells us how the king of Jericho sent a note to Rahab and told her to hand over the spies. Instead of betraying them however, she hid them under stalks of flax. She lied about them and saved their lives by sheer trickery.

Having saved them, she shared with them the feelings and fears of the entire city of Jericho, "your terror is fallen upon us . . . all the inhabitants of the land faint because of you" (verse 9).

Having disclosed the feelings of her people, she then

117

went on to declare her own faith in God. Verses 9 and 11 contain these amazing words from a poor, pagan prostitute, "I know that the LORD hath given you the land . . . for the LORD your God, he is God in heaven above, and in earth beneath." Notice how unusual is this woman's faith. It seems to have come from nowhere and with no sense of preparation.

On the basis of this faith she then went on to ask for mercy. She wanted the spies to "swear unto me by the LORD . . . that ye will save alive my father, and my mother, and my brethren, and my sisters, and all that they have, and deliver our lives from death" (verses 12, 13). We notice that there is no mention of a husband or children. It appears as though she was thinking only of others.

The two Israelite spies agreed to her request on two conditions. The first was that she should be silent on what had been done, and the second, that "when we come into the land, thou shalt bind this line of scarlet thread in the window which thou didst let us down by" (verse 18).

This remarkable woman then outlined a plan of escape and return to camp for the two men. Finally, when they had departed, she demonstrated the quality of her faith by binding the scarlet line in her window immediately.

Rahab confessed her faith in verse 11, but she demonstrated her faith in verse 21. The spies had said, *when we come into the land,* but her faith was such that she expected them at any time.

We meet Rahab again in Joshua 6. In this chapter we read of the complete destruction of Jericho. Verse 21 says, "And they utterly destroyed all that was in the city, both man and woman, young and old, and ox, and sheep, and ass, with the edge of the sword." The entire city was destined for annihilation. Rahab, along with her family, should have met the same fate. She was, in one sense, as good as dead. However, verse 22 tells how Joshua sent the same two men saying, "Go into the harlot's house, and bring out thence the woman, and all that she hath, as ye sware unto her."

Verse 23 tells how the young men went and brought out Rahab and her kindred and all that she had and, "left them without the camp of Israel." We can't help but notice that Rahab's testimony was better than Lot's was at Sodom. Genesis 19:12 tells how the angels "said unto Lot, Hast thou here any besides? son in law, and thy sons, and thy daughters, and whatsoever thou hast in the city, bring them out of this place."

Verse 14 tells how "Lot went out, and spake unto his sons in law ... and said, Up, get you out of this place; for the LORD will destroy this city. But he seemed as one that mocked unto his sons in law."

Whatever it was that Rahab said, her family all believed her and so they shared her deliverance.

Verse 25 of Joshua 6 contains two important facts concerning Rahab, "And Joshua saved Rahab the harlot alive ... and she dwelleth in Israel even unto this day." She might have been saved to continue as a poor, pagan prostitute, to be a creature of no importance, never to be heard of again. But the outstanding fact here is that she was *saved alive*. She was saved to live—not saved so as by fire, but saved from the dead and then saved to continue a new and more wonderful life—*and she dwelleth in Israel even unto this day*.

Now let us observe an amazing thing that happened to her when she began this new quality of life and what the Bible has to say concerning her.

Matthew 1:1-16 is "The book of the generation of Jesus Christ." It is the list of those from whom, and through whom, the Lord Jesus Christ was born in the flesh. In one sense it is the Royal Line and these names are those in the Royal Family. Verse 5 reads, "And Salmon begat Booz of Rachab; and Booz begat Obed of Ruth; and Obed begat Jesse; And Jesse begat David the king."

The spellings are slightly changed in two of the names, but the characters are the same. It should read, "And Salmon begat Boaz of Rahab; and Boaz begat Obed of Ruth."

We thus find that Rahab didn't disappear when she was saved. She was saved to live—and what a life she had! She married Salmon. Just think what a remarkable woman she must have been! She was a pagan, she was penniless, and she was a known prostitute, yet something about her drew her to Salmon and he married her. It is possible that Salmon was a wealthy man for his son Boaz was.

Rahab had a son, and his name was Boaz. It is this same Boaz we meet in the book of Ruth. As we consider how kindly Boaz dealt with this poor pagan girl named Ruth, who was already a widow, we remember that his mother had also been a poor, pagan girl without a husband to care for her.

Remember also how kind Rahab had been to the spies when they were in need in Jericho. The man Boaz was gracious and kind because he had that kind of a mother. Rahab still lived on through Boaz.

It is also a lovely thought to consider Rahab in relationship to Ruth. Ruth had one mother-in-law whom she loved called Naomi. She got another mother-in-law when she married Boaz, and this was Rahab.

We read in Ruth 4:16 how, when Ruth had her son, called Obed, "Naomi took the child, and laid it in her bosom, and became nurse unto it." It is a happy thought to consider that Rahab was the other grandmother, that she, too, may have held little Obed in her arms. She who should have perished in the flames at Jericho lived on in Boaz and Obed. Later she lived on in Jesse and then in David.

The greatest miracle of all is to realize that through her were descended both Joseph and Mary, "of whom was born Jesus, who is called Christ" (Matthew 1:16). The thought is so immense, so challenging, so completely beyond human understanding, that when Rahab was saved to live, she was saved so that one day there might be a Mary, *of whom was born Jesus, who is called Christ.*

This is indeed the highest point of Rahab's history, but it is not the end of her story in the Bible. The "Book of Rahab" begins in the Old Testament and reaches into the New Testament. In the New Testament it reaches into the gospels, and into the epistles also.

Hebrews 11 is the great chapter on faith. "Now faith is the substance of things hoped for, the evidence of things not seen." In its forty verses are gathered the heroes of faith, the men and women, chosen from all history, as the finest representatives of faith in action. We meet such heroes as Enoch, Abraham, Isaac, Jacob and other giants of the Old Testament.

But verse 31 reads, "By faith the harlot Rahab perished not with them that believed not, when she had received the spies in peace." Here we find this amazing woman again, still linked with the word harlot. This time she is set forth as one of the heroes of faith—chosen from the ranks of Jewish history.

There is only one other woman in this eleventh chapter mentioned as a special example of faith. Verse 11 records, "Through faith also Sara herself received strength." What a comparison these two make—Sara and Rahab! Rahab was a prostitute, and the name Sara means "princess." So we have the princess and the prostitute chosen to represent faith that honored God and magnified Him in all His purposes.

If we stop and consider that this epistle was written to the Hebrews, of all people, we can realize in a new way the dignity that must have been attached to the name Rahab. What a far cry it was from the fires of blazing Jericho to the fame of God's holy Word!

But even this is not the end of Rahab in the New Testament. We meet her again in the epistle of James. This becomes increasingly fascinating when we remember that James was the one who emphasized the need of works, as well as faith. James 2:20 so challenges us, "But wilt thou know, O vain man, that faith without works is dead?" James sets out to prove the absolute necessity of works to vindicate and substantiate the profession of faith.

To illustrate his point he chooses two great characters from Jewish history. In James 2:21-24 he speaks of Abraham as a man justified by works *and not by faith only*. Then in verse 25 he writes, "Likewise also was not Rahab the harlot justified by works, when she received the messengers, and had sent them out another way?" Fancy putting Rahab alongside Abraham, as the two chosen ones! What a woman! What a testimony she had! The former pagan prostitute becomes the example for all people to follow—not only because of her faith but also because of her works. No wonder Joshua 6:25 says, "she dwelleth in Israel even unto this day." She does so, in many different ways.

We have noted as we have read the Scriptures that this wonderful woman is constantly referred to as Rahab the harlot. The name goes with her everywhere—except in one place. It is such a delightful gesture and such a blessed comfort to look in Matthew 1:1-16 and find that when it comes to the Royal Line she is noted without that title. In verse 5 she is just Rahab, the lady who was the wife of Salmon, the lady whose son became the grandfather of the great King David. There she stands in all her honor and dignity—and how truly she deserved it.

This then is "The Book of Rahab" which illustrates for us, in a unique way, the twofold work of God for the believer.

Rahab was due to perish in Jericho, but she was saved. However, her salvation didn't end with her escape from death—she was saved to live. The wonder of her life was that God's purposes were fully accomplished through her.

This should mean something to us when we remember that I Corinthians 10 is telling us to work at these stories and learn lessons for today.

Are you saved? Were you also saved to live? Is your life so yielded to Christ that by your faith and through your works the purposes of God are being fully accomplished through you? How is the "Book of You" developing?

A Prayer for Meditation

Dear Father, this story challenges my heart.

Rahab had so little and I have so much. Yet she did so much and I do so little.

Forgive me, Father, for my selfishness and lack of vision.

May I be bold in my faith and step out fearlessly into a future unknown to me but perfectly clear to my Saviour.

May my works be such that people will take knowledge of me, that I have been with Jesus—and, best of all, that Jesus is always with me. In His name. Amen.

CHAPTER 10

THE POWER OF CHRISTIAN MATURITY

WE HAVE BEEN THINKING much, thus far, around the theme of growing up in the Christian faith. We have seen the many areas of need in the Church today where there is an overdisplay of spiritual babyhood. We have considered the peril of immaturity, and then we have gone on to see, in the Old and New Testaments, what is involved in being a mature Christian.

We have read in Hebrews 6:1, "let us go on to perfection [maturity] and in Colossians 1:28, "warning every man, and teaching every man in all wisdom; that we may present every man perfect [mature] in Christ Jesus."

Our minds have been examining the teaching of the Bible so that we can face up to our responsibility in this matter.

What we need now is some basic thinking on the mechanics of Christian maturity. The previous nine chapters have presented us with the truth. How then can this truth become real in my daily experience?

This is the purpose of this chapter with its title, "The Power of Christian Maturity."

We will begin by reading Ephesians 4:1-13 and considering it in the light of our present theme—maturity made real in my own experience.

Verse 1 opens with an immediate challenge, "I therefore, the prisoner of the Lord, beseech you that ye walk worthy of the vocation wherewith ye are called." Notice the phrase *walk worthy*. This is an apt description of maturity in action. Another translation for *walk worthy* is, *that ye walk perfectly balanced*.

This phrase *perfectly balanced* is most descriptive. We can understand the full meaning of it if we consider one of the expensive watches that are available today. Some of these watches are almost miracles of minute engineering. The quality of the precision craftsmanship is such that the movement is practically "perfectly balanced," which means that wherever the watch goes— high in space, or down in the depths of the sea—it keeps perfect time. Whatever the temperature, from blazing heat to arctic cold, its behavior is always the same. As long as it is worn it needs no winding, no attention of any kind. It is made to do a special job and it does it in any, and all, circumstances.

If these descriptions are translated into terms of human experiences—pressures and tensions—the high, the low, the heat and the cold—then the personality which is "perfectly balanced," and continues so to be, is exhibiting all the marks of a mature Christian. This is what the Church needs so much in these days of spiritual irresponsibility.

Verses 2 and 3 give a simple description of what this maturity looks like in terms of human relationships, "Living as becomes you—with complete lowliness of mind (humility) and meekness (unselfishness, gentleness, mildness), with patience, bearing with one another *and* making allowances because you love one another. Be eager *and* strive earnestly to guard *and* keep the harmony *and* oneness of [produced by] the Spirit in the binding power of peace" (*Amplified Bible*).

The verses which follow dwell on the oneness of our faith which comes from the "One God and Father of all, who is above all, and through all, and in you all" (verse 6).

Verses 7-12 speak of the gifts that have come to us

125

through Christ. Verse 11 teaches us that some of these gifts were men, doing specific ministries, "apostles; ... prophets; ... evangelists; ... pastors and teachers; For the perfecting of the saints." The word *perfecting* here means the *complete adjusting*.

Verse 13 is the key verse which tells us why all this was done and all these were given, "Till we all come in the unity of the faith, and of the knowledge of the Son of God, unto a perfect man, unto the measure of the stature of the fullness of Christ." Notice the words *a perfect man*. This is the same word again denoting *a mature man*.

We notice also that it is the *knowledge of the Son of God* that will bring us to maturity.

The *Amplified Bible* gives added insight into this tremendous verse, "until we all attain oneness in the faith and in the comprehension of the full and accurate knowledge of the Son of God; that [we might arrive] at really mature manhood—the completeness of personality which is nothing less than the standard height of Christ's own perfection—the measure of the stature of the fullness of the Christ, *and* the completeness found in Him."

This is something we can dig into, something we can make our own, *really mature manhood . . . completeness of personality . . . the measure of the stature of the fullness of Christ.*

This verse is teaching us a new way to spell out the meaning of Christian maturity. It speaks of a *completeness of personality* and the *fullness of Christ*. We can put these two thoughts together now and see what they mean in terms of our own personal experience.

The word personality is a term well understood by us. It denotes what a person really is. It is that impression we remember as we think of our friends and associates. We do not usually bring to mind the physical features of those remembered; we think in terms of their disposition, their attractiveness, their wholesome-ness—all the characteristics which draw us to one another.

This is good, in many respects, because some, who can make no claims to physical beauty, have such a sweet radiance of personality that the light that shines from within dissolves the shadow that shows without.

But our verse here is speaking about completeness of personality, thus teaching that it is possible to have an incompleteness of personality. It is in this area that the mechanics of Christian maturity operate, and it is here that immaturity is evident.

The human personality is that which is called, in the Bible, the *heart of man*. There are many verses in the Old and New Testaments where the writer or speaker refers to the *heart of man* or the *heart*. When this is done the object is to indicate the human personality—the man who lives within the human body.

The Bible also uses the word *soul* to denote the *heart* or the personality. I Thessalonians 5:23 says, "I pray God your whole spirit and soul and body be preserved blameless unto the coming of our Lord Jesus Christ." Here is direct teaching concerning the trinity of man. In Genesis 1:26 we read, "And God said, Let us make man in our image, after our likeness." Verse 27 continues, "So God created man in his own image, in the image of God created he him."

This does not mean that man resembled God physically because *God is a Spirit*. But the God who said *Let us*, was the triune God, the One whom we worship as the Trinity. Man was made in the image and after the likeness of the triune God—the Trinity, so he was created as a "human trinity"—spirit, soul and body.

Man has a human spirit whereby he is able to have fellowship and union with God. He has a human soul, or heart, or personality by which he can have fellowship and union with those around him. He has a human body which is the vehicle through which these fellowships can be demonstrated, enjoyed and fulfilled.

Our verse in Ephesians 4:13 is thus pointing us to *really mature manhood—the completeness of personality which is nothing less than the standard height of Christ's own perfection,* a maturity based on completeness.

The author of Psalm 119 also had this thought in mind. In verse 2 he says, "Blessed are they that keep his testimonies, and that seek him with the whole heart." Notice that the *blessedness* comes when the *whole heart* is involved—the completeness of personality.

In verse 10 we read, "With my whole heart have I sought thee." In verse 34 the longing for maturity is shown, "Give me understanding, and I shall keep thy law; yea, I shall observe it with my whole heart." His sincerity is seen in verse 58, "I intreated thy favour with my whole heart." His determination is in evidence in verse 69, "I will keep thy precepts with my whole heart." Verse 145 reveals the depth of his hunger for God, "I cried with my whole heart."

What we need, therefore, is a *whole heart* experience, a *completeness of personality* that will lead us to *really mature manhood.*

The Bible also teaches that the human heart—or the personality—can be divided into three areas—the emotions, the mind or intellect, and the will. In Matthew 15:19 the Lord Jesus said, "For out of the heart proceed evil thoughts, murders, adulteries, fornications, thefts, false witness, blasphemies." All the sordid emotional actions and reactions come from the human heart —or personality.

In John 14:1 and 27 the Lord said, "Let not your heart be troubled." Emotional fear and distress are experienced in the human heart—or personality.

In Matthew 9:4 we read, "And Jesus knowing their thoughts said, Wherefore think ye evil in your hearts?" Mark 2:8 records, "And immediately when Jesus perceived in his spirit that they so reasoned within themselves, he said unto them, Why reason ye these things in your hearts?" The human heart, or personality, is thus shown as the center also of the mind or the intellect.

The whole of the Book of Daniel became possible because of 1:8, "But Daniel purposed in his heart." Daniel made a decision, and by his act of will he demonstrated the quality of his maturity, even though he was a young man. Notice that the decision was made *in his heart*. The human heart is thus the place where the will is exercised.

We can now begin to see that the phrase *completeness of personality* has a depth of meaning which can come as an immediate challenge to our hearts and lives. Ephesians 4:13 speaks of *the measure of the stature of the fullness of the Christ*. This signifies that *really mature manhood* and *completeness of personality* result from the *fullness of Christ*. Inasmuch as Christ is allowed to *fill me*, in that much do I experience a growing completeness of personality.

This is something akin to the phrase we read in Ephesians 5:18, "And be not drunk with wine, wherein is excess; but be filled with the Spirit." To be filled with the Spirit does not mean or imply that I get more of the Spirit for I already have the Spirit. But it does mean that the indwelling Spirit gets more of me. As I open up my heart, or personality, to His entrance—as I yield myself to His will—then He can fill more of me. As He fills more of me, then I have more of Him.

Remember always that to be filled with the Spirit is to be controlled by the Spirit. What I yield He fills. What He fills He controls. Therefore, being filled with the Spirit leads to discipline and control—as Ephesians 5:18 indicates—and not to *excess*.

Remember, also, that the Lord Jesus said in John 16:13, 14, "Howbeit when he, the Spirit of truth, is come, he will guide you into all truth: for he shall not speak of himself . . . He shall glorify me." The proof of a Spirit-filled life is the fact that Christ is uplifted and glorified in the life of the believer.

Any claim to *being filled with the Holy Spirit* which is not backed up by a Christ-centered and Christ-exalting life is something different from the teaching of the Word of God.

We are considering in this chapter the mechanics of Christian maturity. What is the power, and how does it operate? How can I be a mature Christian? What does it involve when it is spelled out letter by letter?

At this stage we can begin to answer the questions we have been asking. Christian maturity does not come naturally—by age, experience, education or church office. I do not become mature by praying for it and agonizing for it. Nor do I reach this position by extended Bible study, or by reading books on victorious Christian living, or by attending "Deeper Life Conferences," or "Keswick Conventions."

Christian maturity comes from completeness of personality which itself is the result of the fullness of Christ. My heart, or personality, consists of the three areas that make up "me"—my emotions, my mind or intellect, and my will. As the Lord Jesus Christ, through His Holy Spirit, is allowed to move into these three areas and fill them, so I experience a growing sense of His fullness. The measure of His fullness is the measure of my maturity, regardless of my age, race, education or experience.

Remember always that the evidence of His filling is the evidence of His control. Where He fills, He controls. Where I control, He cannot fill. Where He cannot fill or control, then I cannot experience real maturity.

Many Christians are incomplete in their own life by their lack of knowledge concerning these three areas—the emotions, the mind or intellect, and the will.

My relationship to Christ must begin through the emotional side of my personality. This is so because every relationship I have, or experience, or make, begins on an emotional basis. There is nothing wrong with being emotionally moved in my response to Christ—it is both natural and to be expected.

Some people miss so much by being against the Gospel, because they say it is emotional. I have seen some of these same people watching an exciting football game. Their emotional response and involvement was magnificent to behold. In fact their enjoyment of the game could be measured by the emotions they displayed. There is nothing wrong with this—this is the way we are made.

These same people insist that our relationship to God should be on the intellectual level and, in this, they are perfectly correct. But to insist on the intellectual only, to the exclusion of the emotional is unfair and unnatural. I need to know the rules to understand the football game, but mere intellectual appreciation does not make a respectable citizen stand and cheer in response to a brilliant play.

The difficulty arises when the emotional side of the personality is stressed and encouraged to the exclusion of the mind or intellect and the will. The *whole heart* is the unity of the three areas. The *completeness of personality* is only achieved when each of the three areas is filled with the fullness of Christ.

I have worked with young people for many years. I have enjoyed the sincerity of their singing and the honesty of their words of testimony. I have listened to many a high school and college student telling of his love for the Lord Jesus. I have seen tears flow, as promises were made to love Him and serve Him.

All that was said was absolutely sincere, and an interested listener might be moved to feel that this was the beginning of a wonderful life for Christ. But history proves that this is not always so. There are many disillusioned, disappointed and dissatisfied Christians today in our churches. Yet, at one time they spoke brave, sincere words for Jesus.

131

The answer is basically simple. Sincerity is not enough. An emotional response is necessary, but, if that is all there is, then there can never be a growth to maturity. The whole heart means every area yielded to Christ.

It is often easy to be emotionally moved. Emotions cost nothing. In fact, a good emotional response to Christ can often draw special attention to the one involved. My exalting of my love for Christ could even result in my exalting of myself.

I start to grow when I sit down and count the cost of allowing the Lord Jesus to move into the area of my mind and my intellect. When the Lord Jesus moves into a life He brings His own standards of values and His own orders of priority. He said in Luke 12:15, "A man's life consisteth not in the abundance of the things which he possesseth." The Lord Jesus taught and lived this truth while here on earth. He will still want to live this truth in any heart He indwells. But the world in which we live does not teach this truth. We live in the most materialistic society that has ever existed. We do business against this background. We are taught to think and live without this truth as our guiding star.

Mature Christianity shows itself when new standards emerge and new priorities take over in every area of life. To many Christians this will mean new standards of honesty in school, college, business and home. And, let us be honest, some of us are not willing to allow Christ's standards to be evident in our lives. It may cost me my job, or my career, or my character.

To other Christians, allowing Christ to fill and control the mind or intellect will mean new standards of purity in thought and word and deed. This is where the high school and college student has to count the cost. "Shall I be 'with it,' or 'with Him'?" The test here is really going to hurt. This may cost me my popularity, my girl friend, my boy friend. I may lose the "office" I have been working for in the school organization, or my place on the team.

These new standards of purity will challenge my tastes in clothing, literature, music, art and every other aspect where cultural tastes are evidenced. And, it may cost too much to allow Christ's standards to control me. It may be much easier to let things stay as they are—and just get by with the rest. I don't have to yield full control to Christ, but I will never begin to move into maturity unless I do.

It is good at this point to emphasize that allowing Christ to control is not something to be "endured." I do not have to lose so many "things" that I find myself lonely and bereft of all joy and delight—because God will never be any man's debtor. When Christ comes with His new standards He brings His new satisfaction. I exchange my paltry pleasures for the sheer joyous delight of His presence in my life. It pays a thousand times in this life to love and serve the Lord Jesus, but I may prefer the coinage of this world to the companionship of Christ.

The third area of my personality that Christ wants to fill is the volitional aspect or the will. Incidentally, modern psychology and psychiatry also teach that the human personality consists of these three divisions. Various schools and thinkers use differing names for the three areas, but their teaching is basically that set forth in the Bible—a personality composed of emotions, mind and will.

The will is that decisive part which puts into orbit the reasoning of the mind fired by the enthusiasm of the emotions. It is the finger on the trigger which, when squeezed, commits the owner to a definite line of action. It turns reasoning into reality.

The tragedy is that many Christians can be fired up with emotional enthusiasm; they can reason the thing through and work out a plan of action. However, when it comes to making the final decision they hesitate and finally draw back. As a result, nothing is crystallized. The cause of Christ suffers and in many instances the Christian who draws back soon slips back. Instead of maturity and progress there is the sense of failure that clouds the vision and weakens the witness.

Until Christ fills and controls my will, little of lasting value will emerge from my heart and life. There are Christians at home today who once felt the pull of the mission field. They sensed and were moved by the need and the urgency. They considered, and, led by Christ, they planned how this moving of the Spirit in their lives could lead to missionary training and service. In some cases they even went on to actual training and preparation. But, somewhere along the line, the "will" never fitted into the program. The final thrust was never given, and what could have been so precious and powerful became so pointless and useless.

We have been basing our thinking on Ephesians 4:13 with its vision of *really mature manhood* and *completeness of personality*. Verse 14 goes on to enjoin us, "That we henceforth be no more children, tossed to and fro." Here again is the warning against remaining as a babe in Christ. How true are these words today—*tossed to and fro!*

Verse 17 challenges us to measure ourselves against the world around us, "that ye henceforth walk not as other Gentiles (heathen) walk, in the vanity of their minds." The word *vanity* here means "the folly, the emptiness and the futility of their lives." Spiritual immaturity leads to this very thing—"emptiness and futility."

Verses 18 and 19 present a remarkable picture of the world around us with its darkness, willful blindness, spiritual apathy and utter impurity.

Then verse 20 says, "But ye have not so learned Christ." This is a short, simple verse, but it pulls us up fast. How have you learned Christ? Not learned what

He has done, but come to learn Him—face to face, moment by moment?

In one way, many of us do not know Christ as He is. We know what He has done, and what He has said, and what He will do when He comes again, but we do not have a close intimate knowledge of Him. This can only come as we open up our *whole hearts* to His control.

The rest of Ephesians 4 becomes a wonderful setting forth of what truly happens when there is completeness of personality through the filling of emotions, mind and will. Verse 21 says, "If so be that ye have heard him, and have been taught by him, as the truth is in Jesus." If this is so, then the results in the Christian experience will be as follows: Verse 23 says there will be a "new mind." Verse 24 adds: "that ye put on the 'new man.'" Verse 25 speaks of a "new membership," *for we are members one of another*.

Verse 27 tells of a "new master," and verse 28 of a "new method." Verse 29 speaks of the "new ministry" we will have—*minister grace unto the hearers*. Verse 31 describes the "new manners" that will be seen when the old life is *put away*.

This is so wonderful and so needed in every church, but it can only come true when Christians see their need, the answer to that need, then act upon it!

The need for Christian maturity is evident. The power to meet that need is present in the person of the indwelling Christ. All that God is waiting for is our willingness to come as the writer in Psalm 119:2 and, "seek him with the whole heart."

A PRAYER FOR MEDITATION

I thank Thee, Heavenly Father, that spiritual maturity is something I can know and experience.

Teach me more about completeness of personality in my own experience.

May my faith go deeper than mere emotionalism and further than excited enthusiasm.

May my mind, intellect and will be involved in my relationship with the Lord Jesus.

Grant me wisdom to see the implications of being filled with Christ, and courage to count the cost.

May I exercise that childlike faith that sees the need, recognizes the provision to meet that need, then acts with humble simplicity to make it real in my own experience. This I pray in the name of my Saviour, the Lord Jesus Christ. Amen.

CHAPTER 11

THE BOOK OF ACHAN—SAVED TO PERISH

WE HAVE BEEN CONSIDERING, in the previous chapters, the glorious possibility of becoming so involved with the Lord Jesus that the complete personality is open to experience His infilling.

Such a step is the sure way to knowing the power of Christian maturity. In one sense, going on with Christ is the natural thing to do. If our hearts desire greater things and better things, then this is the answer, a deeper involvement with the Lord Jesus Christ.

But history and human experience show that a Christian can have this desire, be all set to yield his life to His fullness, and then one utterly stupid, unnecessary act or decision can smash the entire wonderful possibility.

This present chapter, "The Book of Achan," is the awful story of such a foolish act—so stupid and senseless in its doing but so terrible and devastating in its consequences.

We have thought already on the significance of the title, "The Book of Joshua"—what God could do with one man's yielded life. The same thought is seen also in "The Book of Ruth" and "The Book of Daniel," as well as in other such titles. God used men and women to change the course of history. Race and respectability did not count in these operations. All that was necessary was a willingness to be involved with God.

The "Book of Achan" is also the life of Achan. It

began so full of promise, it ended suddenly, so full of judgment.

The "Book of Achan" makes a searching contrast to the "Book of Rahab." Rahab was a pagan, outside the family of God, condemned to perish in the judgment of Jericho—but she was saved. What is more, she was saved to live, and "she dwelleth in Israel even unto this day" (Joshua 6:25). She deserved nothing but condemnation, yet she received only blessing.

Achan was one of God's chosen people. He had been redeemed and preserved and blessed. His days of wandering in the wilderness were over. He had crossed the Jordan. He had shared in the victory at Jericho. He was all set to move into his own inheritance. He had sons and daughters who would live on to perpetuate his memory, so that Achan, too, could continue to dwell in Israel *even unto this day*.

The dark days were over. There was nothing but sunshine and blessing ahead. Then— one stupid, senseless act shattered all that might have been his. His whole world fell to pieces and, in a horrible moment of judgment, he and all that he had vanished forever.

Rahab was saved to live. Achan was saved—only to die and perish. Rahab dwelleth in Israel even to this day, but Achan perished with his whole family and possessions. He remains only as an awful warning and an ugly memory. There was nothing left but a heap of stones and the wisps of smoke rising from the burning.

What a wasted life, when all could have been so different! What challenge and a warning to every child of God! We have been saved to live, but we, too, can be saved to "perish." Not that we lose our eternal salvation purchased by the blood of Christ at Calvary. That is ours. But, all that we might be in wholesome witness, and all that might come from our yielded lives, can be utterly crushed and swept away through a stupid, useless, senseless act or decision. The warning is clear and plain.

We have considered, elsewhere, that names in the Bible can have a special significance, indicating in a way the character of the one so named. This becomes apparent when we consider the names given in Joshua 7:1. Here are shown for us the four generations that ended with Achan. First we have his great-grandfather whose name was Zerah. This name means "a sprout," or "a shoot," indicating the development of a new life and a new beginning.

Next comes Achan's grandfather whose name is given as Zabdi. This name means "God is endower," or "God is the giver." This comes as a natural progression from the new beginning.

The father's name was Carmi, meaning "fruitful and noble," thus showing how "the shoot" was fulfilling the promise.

Then comes Achan, and here the name sequence ends, for Achan means "trouble." This was the name given to him at his birth, and how significant it was for the days ahead.

Thus we have four generations leading on from blessing to blessing and then an abrupt stop—all that might have been, failed to mature. Achan had sons, but their names are not known. There was no need to know who they were for they perished with their father. The shoot that held such hopes for the future was suddenly cut off.

The purpose of the story of Achan is to see the extent of the repercussions that came from his one stupid act. Not only did Achan and his entire family suffer as a result, but also the entire nation. Such a thing can still happen today when a man's stupid folly affects not only his family, but also his church and the witness of God's people in that place.

We see this illustrated in Joshua 7:1, "But the children of Israel committed a trespass in the accursed thing." In one way this does not seem fair, for only Achan was the offender--the rest of his family were completely innocent. But a little research into the story reveals several significant statements.

In Deuteronomy 7 Moses was telling the people God's plans for the entry into Canaan. Remember that the Book of Deuteronomy was the "post mortem" on the wilderness failure. In 1:1 we read, "These be the words which Moses spake unto all Israel on this side Jordan in the wilderness." These words would be fresh in the ears of all the Israelites.

In Deuteronomy 7:23 we read, "But the LORD thy God shall deliver them unto thee . . . he shall deliver their kings into thine hand. . . . The graven images of their gods shall ye burn with fire: thou shalt not desire the silver or gold that is on them . . . Neither shalt thou bring an abomination into thine house, lest thou be a cursed thing like it: but thou shalt utterly detest it, and thou shalt utterly abhor it; for it is a cursed thing."

The word "accursed" which is used here and later on, means "destined and dedicated for destruction." See the significance of this in verse 26, "lest thou be a cursed thing like it." The teaching was clear—anyone who identified himself with an unholy, evil thing condemned to destruction would also be identified in that destruction.

Note also the words in verse 25 whereby the children of Israel had not "to desire the silver or gold" that was on the images of the pagan gods.

Achan deliberately went against this teaching that he himself had heard from the lips of Moses.

Then in Joshua 6:17-19 Joshua gave strict instructions regarding Jericho, "The city shall be accursed, even it, and all that are therein, to the LORD . . . And ye, in any wise keep yourselves from the accursed thing, lest ye make yourselves accursed, when ye take of the accursed thing, and make the camp of Israel a curse, and trouble it. But all the silver, and gold . . . are consecrated unto the LORD."

These words were heard by Achan hours before his

foolish heart rebelled. There was the warning—
everything in Jericho was accursed and to be burned—
if a man took anything, then the curse would fall on
him and he would be burned. In taking the accursed
thing he would bring a curse on the whole camp and
everyone would suffer. Nothing could be plainer or
more simple to understand. In spite of this, Achan took
a Babylonian garment, two hundred shekels of silver,
and a wedge of gold (Joshua 7:21).

Why did he do it? Why do Christians do stupid
things today that bring shame on their families and the
stain of dishonor on their church? Undoubtedly Achan
fell a victim once more to the wiles of Satan. We read
in I John 2:16, "For all that is in the world, the lust of
the flesh, and the lust of the eyes, and the pride of life,
is not of the Father, but is of the world." This is the
devil's trinity of temptation, his one means of attack on
the children of men.

We see the Satanic attack first in Genesis 3:6, "And
when the woman saw that the tree was good for food,
and that it was pleasant to the eyes, and a tree to be
desired to make one wise, she took of the fruit thereof"
—the lust of the flesh, the lust of the eyes, the pride of
life.

Here the enemy scored the first of his many victories
in human hearts. He was able to do this with the
woman because she had previously listened to the insin-
uation of Satan. She had said in verse 3, "God hath
said, Ye shall not eat of it, neither shall ye touch it, lest
ye die." To which Satan had added his denial, "Ye
shall not surely die" (verse 4).

Satan had made his greatest lie in saying, "Sin—and
you can get away with it." This is what he has been
saying all down the ages—"Go on, sin! You won't die,
you can get away with it!" Both the man and woman
listened to the devil in Genesis 3 and this became the
fall of man, when man openly rebelled against his
Creator and believed the lie of the devil.

141

This is what Achan did. He heard all the warnings. He knew what would happen. He walked into the situation with his eyes wide open. He knew his family would perish, and that Israel would suffer. He knew it—but he did not believe it! He thought he could get away with it—just this once.

This is the story behind so much failure in so many Christian lives. We know what the Bible says, but we think we can get away with it. We read in Galatians 6:7, "Be not deceived; God is not mocked: for whatsoever a man soweth, that shall he also reap," but we rationalize ourselves out of the verse and out of the verdict.

This is why the story of Achan is so important at this stage of our study in this book. Remember always, that I Corinthians 10:1-12 directs us to measure our own lives against these specific stories in the Old Testament, "wherefore let him that thinketh he standeth take heed lest he fall" (verse 12). In spite of our longings and desires for Christian maturity there is always the awful possibility of failure such as Achan experienced. Sincerity is no protection against sin.

Joshua 7 makes miserable reading. The shadow of Achan falls across the words as we read them. The amazing thing is to see how quickly the words of Joshua 6:18 came true, "And ye, in any wise keep yourselves from the accursed thing, lest ye make yourselves accursed, when ye take of the accursed thing, and make the camp of Israel a curse, and trouble it." The camp of Israel did become a curse and there was trouble, but no one knew why, except Achan.

Joshua had been greatly encouraged by the initial victory at Jericho. Israel had won their first great battle, and the hearts of the people were rejoicing with growing confidence. Verses 2-4 of chapter 7 tell of this confidence as the men prepared to attack Ai.

They had viewed the situation. They made their plans for using two or three thousand men. They moved in to attack, expecting nothing but victory—and then came utter tragedy, "and they fled before the men of Ai. And the men of Ai smote of them about thirty and six men: for they chased them ... wherefore the hearts of the people melted, and became as water" (verse 5). How descriptive is that phrase, their hearts *became as water.*

In a moment all their confidence vanished. When their hearts melted, their courage evaporated and their hopes vanished. Verse 6 tells how, "Joshua rent his clothes, and fell to the earth upon his face before the ark of the LORD until the eventide, he and the elders of Israel."

Here was God's man to whom had been given "the promise, the program and the power." He had been promised, "Every place ... every day," and now he was stunned into silence.

As Joshua and the people of Israel agonized concerning this awful tragedy, bewildered and crushed with defeat, only one man knew the cause. Achan waited in trembling suspense.

Joshua's first reaction was to blame God. In verse 7 his words pour out in accusing admonition, "Alas, O Lord GOD, wherefore hast thou at all brought this people over Jordan, to deliver us into the hands of the Amorites, to destroy us?" He almost accuses God of treachery. Then Joshua spoke the familiar language of defeat, so often heard in the wilderness, "would to God we had been content, and dwelt on the other side of Jordan." What vain words—who could be content in the wilderness?

In verse 8 the blame is put on Israel. In verse 9 Joshua considered the possibility of all the inhabitants of Canaan surrounding Israel and destroying them to "cut off our name from the earth." Then, in a moment of panic, he cries to God, "and what wilt thou do unto thy great name?" Joshua in his own moment of extreme weakness and failure suddenly imagines the panic there must be in heaven. God, as well as Israel, was suddenly in trouble. How was God going to get Himself out of this predicament?

Then God spoke, "Get thee up; wherefore liest thou thus upon thy face?" (verse 10). This was not a time for panic, but for purging out the sin and evil. As we have seen, only Achan was involved in this tragedy, but notice the words of God in verse 11, "Israel hath sinned, and they have also transgressed my covenant . . . for they have even taken of the accursed thing, and have also stolen, and dissembled also, and they have put it even among their own stuff."

The words of Joshua had come true—one man's sin had blighted the nation and caused suffering and loss to thirty-six men. The men who died would leave widows and orphans. This defeat was only the beginning of other tragedies that might follow, unless the problem was dealt with and the trouble stamped out.

Notice the fourfold accusation that God made against the people. First, *they have taken of the accursed thing,* then, *they have stolen.* Third, *they have dissembled also* (dissembled means to lie or deceive), and last, *they have put it even among their own stuff.*

This last point is not unimportant. Remember Moses had said in Deuteronomy 7:26, "Neither shalt thou bring an abomination into thine house, lest thou be a cursed thing like it." By hiding the loot among his own goods, Achan had brought the cursed thing into his tent and into the camp.

Observe how the whole nation was guilty—"they have taken . . . they have stolen"—and yet it was the action of just one man.

Notice how Achan had committed this fourfold offense. The articles taken and hidden were, "a goodly Babylonish garment, and two hundred shekels of silver, and a wedge of gold" (Joshua 7:21). Joshua 6:19 says, "but all the silver, and gold . . . shall come into the treasury of the Lord." So Achan had taken the accursed thing—*a goodly Babylonish garment;* he had also stolen the silver and gold, because that belonged to God. He had lied and deceived, because after the failure at Ai he remained silent, though he was aware of the cause of the defeat. He could have confessed and spared the entire camp the agony of anxious fear. Finally he had brought the cursed thing within the camp of Israel.

The rest of the chapter is the story of the inevitable consequences of sin. How the heart of Achan must have melted as he saw the relentless selection of God at work, as told in verses 16-18. First, the tribe of Judah, then the family of the Zarhites, then the men of Zabdi, then the father of Achan, Carmi, then, finally, the man himself. What a wretched picture Achan must have made that awful morning as he stood there alone in all his failure!

Joshua's words in verse 19 are wonderful, "And Joshua said unto Achan, My son, give I pray thee, glory to the Lord GOD of Israel, and make confession unto him; and tell me now what thou hast done." Achan had one last chance to give glory to God—and he took it!

How miserable it must have seemed in the cold light of day. The messenger ran to Achan's tent, discovered the garment, the silver and the gold and "they took them out of the midst of the tent, and brought them unto Joshua, and unto all the children of Israel, and laid them out before the LORD" (verse 23). What a pitiful sight they must have made—one garment, some silver and a piece of gold. For these a man had gambled away his life, his loved ones, the honor of Israel and the glory of God.

And so Achan died, and all his family and all his cattle. Everything identified with Achan was burned and the funeral pyre was buried under a pile of stones. Verse 26 says, "And they raised over him a great heap of stones unto this day." Notice those pathetic words, *unto this day!*

The same words appear in Joshua 6:25 concerning Rahab, "she dwelleth in Israel even unto this day." Rahab dwells even unto this day, but Achan was destroyed even unto this day. What a comparison! What a catastrophe! Nothing in Achan's experience with God reached maturity. We have only the madness of a stupid moment when Satan tempted and Achan fell.

I Corinthians 10:6 says, "Now these things were our examples, to the intent we should not lust after evil things, as they also lusted." Remember when Paul wrote "we," he included himself. Paul was capable of such failure—so are we.

How near can you get to Christian maturity and yet lose the lot? Ask Achan!

A Prayer for Meditation

Heavenly Father, this is a terrible story—and it is true. Rahab was saved to live—grant that this may be my experience as I go on with God.

Achan was saved to perish—deliver me, O God, from such an awful tragedy.

May I see "sin" as it really is. Preserve me from seeking loot in the spoil of this world.

Keep me close to "the promise—the program—and the power." Keep me close to Thee, through Jesus Christ my Lord. Amen.

CHAPTER 12

THE PURPOSE OF CHRISTIAN MATURITY

As WE COME to this last chapter in the book we will take time to put ourselves once more under the microscope of God.

The previous chapter challenged us with the awful failure of Achan—something which was personal and individual. It was one man alone who caused the tragedy and the heartache.

We saw in chapter 10 that the power for maturity was a completeness of personality where emotions, mind and will were filled with Christ. When the whole heart is "in gear" with Christ, then the power of the risen Lord is experienced in every area of human living —then it is that maturity is seen and known.

We can see the personal aspect of maturity when we examine Paul's letter to the Philippians 3:7-15. Here is a letter written by the most mature Christian who ever lived, a man who demonstrated constantly a unique ability to handle every situation, whether in suffering or in satisfaction.

These nine verses are his personal testimony to his relationship with the risen Lord Jesus. In Philippians 1:21 he wrote, "For to me to live is Christ, and to die is gain." In the verses we are considering he expands that concept and spells out for us the details involved in such a dedication.

These nine verses are essentially personal. Thirteen

147

times he uses the personal pronoun "I" as he tells what his desires are toward the Lord Jesus:

7 But what things were gain to me, those I counted loss for Christ.

8 Yea, doubtless, and I count all things but loss for the excellency of the knowledge of Christ Jesus my Lord: for whom I have suffered the loss of all things, and do count them but dung, that I may win Christ,

9 And be found in him, not having mine own righteousness, which is of the law, but that which is through the faith of Christ, the righteousness which is of God by faith:

10 That I may know him, and the power of his resurrection, and the fellowship of his sufferings, being made conformable unto his death;

11 If by any means I might attain unto the resurrection of the dead.

12 Not as though I had already attained, either were already perfect: but I follow after, if that I may apprehend that for which I am apprehended of Christ Jesus.

13 Brethren, I count not myself to have apprehended: but this one thing I do, forgetting those things which are behind, and reaching forth unto those things which are before,

14 I press toward the mark for the prize of the high calling of God in Christ Jesus.

15 Let us therefore, as many as be perfect, be thus minded.

The important thing here is to read verses 7-14, realize what is involved, and then let verse 15 hit home, "Let us therefore, as many as be perfect, be thus minded." (The word *perfect* is the word "mature," which is the basis of our study in this book.)

We must grasp the fact that this testimony of Paul is not just something we gaze at with holy admiration. We are not to be spectators applauding the mighty deeds of a popular hero. We are to be involved in the same attitudes and aspirations, *let us be thus minded*.

These verses give us the entire purpose of Paul's living, and Paul's purpose must be our purpose, if we want to go on to maturity.

There is tremendous truth, especially in verses 10, 11

and 12. This truth is more fully revealed in the *Amplified Bible:*

> 10 [For my determined purpose is] that I may know Him —that I may progressively become more deeply and intimately acquainted with Him, perceiving and recognizing and understanding [the wonders of His Person] more strongly and more clearly. And that I may in that same way come to know the power outflowing from His resurrection [which it exerts over believers]; and that I may so share His sufferings as to be continually transformed [in spirit into His likeness even] to His death, [in the hope]
>
> 11 That if possible I may attain to the [spiritual and moral] resurrection [that lifts me] out from among the dead [even while in the body]
>
> 12 Not that I have now attained [this ideal] or am already made perfect, but I press on to lay hold of (grasp) *and* make my own, that for which Christ Jesus, the Messiah, has laid hold of me *and* made me His own.

What magnificent words these are. The entire passage radiates a boldness and an outlook which puts to shame the tawdry ambitions of many Christian hearts.

We can understand these verses more clearly if we see that Paul was pressing for a threefold appreciation of the Lord Jesus. His burning desire was to know "the Person—the Power—the Purpose" involved in his relationship with Christ.

If we can make this our own earnest desire then we, too, will be on the pathway of maturity.

Paul's first longing was *that I may know Him.* He was attracted to and fascinated by the "Person" of the Lord Jesus. Ever since that wonderful day—recorded in Acts 9:4,5, when Paul had heard the amazing question, "Saul, Saul, why persecutest thou me?" to which he had stammered out his own question, "Who art thou, Lord?"—he had been filled with an eager desire to know more, so that he could give more.

It is possible to be so taken up with the work of Christ that we discover little of the Person of Christ. I can be meticulously accurate in my doctrine, and yet be

149

vague and uncertain in my personal devotion to my blessed Saviour. To know Him, I must live with Him. There must be a wonderful intimacy between my soul and my Saviour.

This sense of breathless wonder is seen in many of the great hymns of our faith, hymns we love to sing because they touch the chords of our hearts. How much more satisfying when the heart can play its own responsive melody of love and adoration.

This fact of "knowing Him" is something every one of us must pursue if we are to go on, like Paul, to be involved with Him. There is only one way in which we can achieve this experience. It is by spending time with Christ in worship and adoration. The method of spending that time may differ according to our abilities and opportunities, but the necessity is essential. Always remember that worship and adoration are not the same as asking for favors or presenting petitions. Love is often most effective in its silence.

Paul's desire was *to perceive and recognize and understand the wonders of His Person.* Remember that the One whom Paul met on the Damascus Road was the risen Christ in all His power and glory. The One of whom he desired to know more was that same risen Christ, who said in Matthew 28:18, 20, "All power is given unto me in heaven and in earth . . . and, lo, I am with you alway, even unto the end of the world." The Lord had promised His presence; Paul sought to prove His presence.

But there was a purpose in Paul's fervent desire to know the Person of Christ. As he proved His presence so he would experience His power. This is the second great thrust in Philippians 3:10, "And that I may in that same way come to know the power outflowing from His resurrection [which it exerts over believers]" (*Amplified Bible*). The more Paul knew of the Person of Christ, the more he would experience the power of Christ.

150

The greatest need in the Church today is that those who have been redeemed by the blood of Christ should go on to experience the presence of the risen Christ so that they can demonstrate the power of the indwelling Christ—*the power outflowing from His resurrection.*

A knowledge of this will make possible an understanding of verse 11. The King James version reads, *If by any means I might attain unto the resurrection of the dead.* This is both uncertain and ambiguous in communicating the real meaning. The *Amplified Bible* reads, *That if possible I may attain to the [spiritual and moral] resurrection [that lifts me] out from among the dead [even while in the body].* The reference to the resurrection in this verse is not pointing to the dramatic experience of a coming day, but to the outworking day by day of the fact of being born again.

Ephesians 2:1 says, "And you hath he quickened, who were dead in trespasses and sins." We were dead, but now we are alive from the dead. John 5:24 has come true in our experience, "Verily, verily, I say unto you, He that heareth my word, and believeth on him that sent me, hath everlasting life, and shall not come into condemnation; but is passed from death unto life."

When we passed from death unto life we experienced the resurrection referred to in Philippians 3:11. But, notice carefully what Paul is saying in this same verse. He speaks of *a spiritual and moral resurrection.* All Christians have experienced the spiritual resurrection when they were born again. What is so vital now is that the power of the risen Christ that brought the spiritual life should be released, and become operative in the moral life.

It was for this that Paul yearned and pressed forward. It is this that is so much needed in the Church today—the application of the power of Christ to the moral life of the believer. The Lord Jesus said in Matthew 7:20, "Wherefore by their fruits ye shall know them." This is eternal truth applicable to all ages and

151

situations. What a blessed thing it would be if we as believers opened our moral lives more and more to the infusion of the risen Life of Christ.

Such an act would take care of so much of the spiritual junk that clutters up the free-flowing of the Gospel—the pride, the gossip, the backbiting, the jealousy, the impurity in thought, word and deed. All these and the other attendant works of the flesh would be swept away if a moral resurrection took place in our lives.

The aspirations of Paul in II Corinthians 4:10, 11 would then become real in us, "that the life also of Jesus might be made manifest in our body . . . that the life also of Jesus might be made manifest in our mortal flesh." The life of Jesus will be made manifest in our mortal flesh when the power of the risen Christ is made manifest in our moral life.

This can only become true when we, first of all, "know Him" in increasing intimacy, and then know His power at work in our fragile flesh. The moral resurrection will be seen in the growth in Christian maturity as the fragrance of His presence, and power, permeate the complete personality—emotions, mind and will.

The third thing Paul wanted to know is expressed in verse 12, "I press on to lay hold of (grasp) *and* make my own, that for which Christ Jesus, the Messiah, has laid hold of me *and* made me His own" (*Amplified Bible*). When Christ saved Paul, He had a purpose and a plan in mind for Paul's life. Now, what Paul is seeking is that he might be identified with that purpose and that plan.

Knowing "the Person" leads to experiencing "His Power." Yielding my entire life to that "Power" sets in motion the "Purposes" of Christ in my life.

Paul was on the move, he was always "going"—even when he was locked in a prison cell. Remember that the Philippian letter was written in prison, but even there he was "pressing on" and "reaching forth."

Paul saw himself always in relation to the purpose of God. This could be an encouragement to many of us if we went on, so to know the "Purpose" of the "Power" of the "Person" indwelling our hearts and lives, that we saw ourselves caught up in the plans and purposes of God.

If we could see ourselves "in gear" with Christ, then we would know His power "meshed" with the whole of our yielded personality. We could then go on to appreciate that as His "driving power" was experienced in our day by day living, then His plans and purposes would be both set forth and fulfilled through us.

This is what Paul is proclaiming in this personal testimony—something so practical and down to earth, yet something which simply must be experienced if ever the believer is to go on to maturity.

Remember always that "going on" with Christ is not necessarily finding success and "going up" in the world. With Paul, the experience of "going on" with Christ was, in reality, "going down"—but always with Christ.

Then, of course, the point of this passage comes in verse 15, "Let us therefore, as many as be perfect [mature], be thus minded." What Paul said of himself, he says to you and me. His desires must be our desires. His experience must be our experience. We, too, must be able to say, *For my determined purpose is that I may know Him*—the Person—the Power—the Purpose for my life.

Inasmuch as I bow my heart in humble acceptance of this fact, and yield my life to Christ for His outliving, then, in that much, I "grow up" from day to day and Christian maturity becomes my most cherished experience.

A Prayer for Meditation

Heavenly Father, I thank Thee for this testimony of Paul. Help me to know more and more of the glorious Person of my Lord Jesus Christ.

As I know Him, may I understand so much more of His amazing power.

I, too, would desire a moral resurrection within my own personality. Teach me how this can come true in my own experience.

As I grow in grace and maturity may I know more fully Your purposes for my life.

As I understand this plan give me such love in my heart that most gladly will I yield myself in fullest cooperation.

May all this be done for the honor and glory of the Lord Jesus Christ. Amen.